"As an active psychiatrist treating individuals who have trouble 'doing life,' this practical workbook will be my go-to recommendation for them to read. The very simple, both easy-to-read and implement parasympathetic power techniques that Van Dijk teaches, will surely pay off to enhance anyone's interpersonal relationships."

—**Stephen B. Stokl, MD, FRC.P (C)**, assistant (adjunct) professor of psychiatry,
and faculty of medicine at the University of Toronto; and author of *Mentally Speaking*

"Ecstatic to see a workbook written for anyone who feels overwhelmed by intense emotions. Sheri Van Dijk helps the reader understand emotional processes, and how anyone can reduce emotional pain and suffering. Every chapter has rescue skills that are quick and easy to learn and can be used immediately. The tools and handouts can be used over and over whenever difficult emotions arise. Sheri is encouraging and supportive for you to practice and use these skills so that you can experience something different and gain confidence in how these skills work."

—**Lisa Porret, MSc**, registered psychologist in private practice for nearly two decades
with emphasis on clinical psychology

"Sheri Van Dijk's *The DBT Workbook for Emotional Relief* is a practical, coherent guide to understanding intense and often overwhelming emotions. Easy-to-follow worksheets make the array of skills in each chapter accessible and doable! I love how she invites the reader to hopefulness, with practices that affirm our own ability to create positive and pleasurable emotional experiences! I look forward to using this amazing resource myself, and with my clients!"

—**Kinsey Lewis**, registered psychotherapist, and certified trauma specialist with over
twenty-five years of experience in community mental health in Ontario, Canada

"Sheri's workbook outlines a range of very effective tools and strategies that will help you remain compassionate, accepting, and responsive to your own needs in moments when you feel overwhelmed. Her workbook is easy to understand and provides the reader with good examples of how to effectively implement these tools."

—**Sabrina Tuzi, MSW, RSW**, adult crisis worker at Southlake Regional Health Centre

T0274022

"Intense emotional responses that leave you feeling out of control and often alienated can feel impossible to navigate. This workbook is a must-read for anyone who is looking for skills that are quick and effective in finding relief and reclaiming control over their emotions."

—**Jodi-Lyn Knoop, MSW, RSW**, psychotherapist, and founder and CEO of Turning Stones Therapy

"The DBT Workbook for Emotional Relief is one of Sheri's best. The book is filled with insightful DBT exercises and self-assessment work to help you get through emotional pain and distress. I'm looking forward to suggesting this book to all my clients and those in the mental health care profession."

—**Jackson Yee**, health coach/teacher

"In this workbook, Van Dijk offers us an incredibly insightful and compassionate guide to understanding and managing difficult emotions. Whether you're struggling to manage your emotions or looking to optimize the skills you already have to thrive, this workbook is written with you in mind. It's simple to follow and is written with clarity and precision to help you through every step in the process of cultivating well-being."

—**Zainib Abdullah, MSW, RSW, RYT**, cofounder and clinical director
at Wellnest Psychotherapy Services in Toronto, ON, Canada

"This book interweaves theory and practice into an invitation to be curious and explore our personal challenges at a flexible pace. It succeeds with integrating the many components of DBT in a manner that both introduces and expands the reader's understanding of emotion regulation. Sheri reminds us that regulation is a 'skill,' and there are times we all need more practice. The reader finds permission to explore the contributors to their emotional dysregulation, and a variety exercises that help to restore balance. The 'Rescue Skills' provided offer an opportunity to deepen our experience of the material, while offering a tool for the times we feel overwhelmed."

—**Leanne M. Garfinkel, MA, SEP, RP**, in private practice in Uxbridge, ON, Canada

"In this quintessential workbook, Sheri Van Dijk dives into integrative DBT strategies for both practitioners and clients alike. Throughout, one will discover novel, practical, and effective approaches to break free of old patterns, gain personal clarity, and experience emotional relief. The masterful use of realistic vignettes validates the human experience and motivates the reader to implement practices for lasting change."

—**Ita Tobis, MSW, RSW**, clinical trauma therapist, and
director of campus programming for Courage 2 Change

THE DBT WORKBOOK FOR EMOTIONAL RELIEF

Fast-Acting Dialectical Behavior Therapy Skills to Balance Out-of-Control Emotions & Find Calm Right Now

SHERI VAN DIJK, MSW

New Harbinger Publications, Inc.

NEW HARBINGER PUBLICATIONS is a registered trademark of New Harbinger Publications, Inc.

New Harbinger Publications is an employee-owned company.

Copyright © 2022 by Sheri Van Dijk
New Harbinger Publications, Inc.
5720 Shattuck Avenue
Oakland, CA 94609
www.newharbinger.com

Cover design by Amy Shoup

Acquired by Tesilya Hanauer

Edited by James Lainsbury

Library of Congress Cataloging-in-Publication Data

Names: Van Dijk, Sheri, author.
Title: The DBT workbook for emotional relief : fast-acting dialectical behavior therapy skills to balance out-of-control emotions and find calm right now / Sheri Van Dijk.
Description: Oakland, CA : New Harbinger Publications, 2022. | Includes bibliographical references.
Identifiers: LCCN 2022000751 | ISBN 9781684039647 (trade paperback)
Subjects: LCSH: Dialectical behavior therapy.
Classification: LCC RC489.D48 V36 2022 | DDC 616.89/142--dc23/eng/20220217
LC record available at https://lccn.loc.gov/2022000751

Printed in the United States of America

26   25   24

10   9   8   7   6   5   4   3   2

For all of the people who have included me on their journey: I'm grateful for the privilege, I applaud your courage, and I admire your strength.

For Marsha Linehan and her team, who created DBT: I'm inspired by your work and thankful for the healing it's allowed me to bring to my own clients.

For my family: as always, thank you for your love and support.

Contents

Introduction

Your work hours have been cut back and you're worrying about what this will mean for your future. Or the kids need help with their homework while your partner is asking you what's for dinner and your boss is demanding that you forward a document they need even though the workday is technically over. Suddenly you find yourself bursting into tears and struggling to breathe. Or the dog just tracked mud all over the floor again and you lose it, yelling at them, and two minutes later you're beating yourself up for tearing a strip off poor sweet Fido. Or your best friend had to cancel the plans you had for this evening and it's the last straw: you're feeling let down and, not knowing what to do with these feelings, you stuff them, perhaps using your favorite substance (food, alcohol, pot…) to help you do so. Sound familiar?

While these specific scenarios might not exactly hit home for you, chances are if you're reading these words you need help with the overwhelming emotions you feel…*Now!* Good news: this book is full of tools that are going to help! In fact, let me give you one right now.

The somatic therapy organization Bodynamic International developed this exercise:

> First, take a deep breath; as you focus on inhaling, press your big toes into the floor; and as you exhale, press your little toes into the floor. Now, out loud (If you can!), say to yourself, "I see…," and name five things you see around you: "I see the lamp, I see the dog, I see the tissue box," and so on. Repeat the breathing, inhaling as you press your big toes into the floor, exhaling as you press your little toes into the floor.

Congratulations, you've just learned a skill that can help you break free of the pattern of reactive behavior that strong emotions can set you on and get on a healthier path to managing those emotions! If you didn't find this exercise particularly helpful, don't worry, there are lots more to come, and you're bound to find some helpful tools in this book. It's important to know that skills like this won't *solve* the problems that cause the emotional distress you feel, but they will help you get unhijacked from the emotion so you can figure out what to do next, while remaining calm and collected rather than stressed, anxious, or chaotic. But before we get into more of these fast-acting skills that will help you solve problems and change emotions in the long run, allow me to tell you a bit more about this book and how it will help, and what you can expect from it.

What Is Emotion Dysregulation?

While we'll never have complete control over our emotions, we can learn to manage them more effectively. You may have heard of *emotion dysregulation*, which occurs when people haven't developed the skills to manage emotions in healthy ways—such as the ability to recognize that they're having an emotional response, to understand why, and to accept it instead of trying to get rid of it or judging themselves for what they're feeling. Emotion dysregulation unfolds in three steps:

1. First, there's a trigger: This could be an external event (like the dog tracking mud into the house), or an internal experience (feeling an emotion; having a memory or image pop into your head; or noticing a physical sensation, such as your heart racing). In response to this trigger, emotions and thoughts arise: for instance, you feel frustrated about the mud on the floor and you judge the dog; your interpretation of the emotion, or the picture that popped into your head, causes you to feel angry; or you start to worry about the change in your heart rate, wondering if you're having a heart attack.

2. Next, your body joins the party: Perhaps your heart rate increases or starts to beat harder, your muscles tense up, and hormones like cortisol (the "stress hormone") and adrenaline (associated with the fight-or-flight response) kick in. Your facial expression and body language will also change to reflect your emotions, and you'll probably experience urges that go along with this as well (like the urge to yell at Fido).

3. Finally, in response to what you're feeling you engage in a behavior, like yelling at the dog, bursting into tears, or pushing your emotions away to avoid them.

It's important for you to know that *everyone* gets dysregulated at times! When stress increases and we get overwhelmed, it gets harder to manage emotions skillfully. For example, as the world was seeing the first pandemic in a hundred years, I was moving my office, clients were canceling out of fear of the virus, and one of my dogs had to have surgery. (He's fine!) I was practicing all sorts of emotion regulation skills and still bursting into tears at times! This is emotion dysregulation. It happens to all of us at times, and it looks different for everyone.

Many people learn emotion regulation skills as they grow up, and for many people managing their emotions becomes a natural process. But there are times when things get especially distressing and we have to consciously put more effort into managing emotions. And of course, some of us were never taught healthy ways of managing emotions in the first place. There are essentially two categories of behaviors that are unskillful when it comes to dealing with strong emotions: overcontrolling and undercontrolling.

Overcontrol and Undercontrol

People who tend to *overcontrol* bottle things up or stuff emotions. Sometimes this is related to a sense that it's not safe to express emotions, or they may think that having or expressing feelings makes them "weak," or that they "shouldn't" feel that way. As a result, overcontrollers try to hide their feelings from others, which can lead to a sense of disconnection from the people around them; feelings of shame and other painful emotions can also arise. Unfortunately, overcontrolling emotions will eventually lead to problems: perhaps you'll blow up in a way that has negative consequences for you and the people around you. (You can only stuff it down for so long before you blow!) Or you might act in passive-aggressive ways that others won't tolerate for long. Or you may just end up feeling lonely and isolated in the long run.

At the other end of the spectrum are the people who are undercontrolled. If you're undercontrolled, some of your go-to behaviors might be blowing up when you're feeling angry, crying easily with various emotions, or engaging in more problematic behaviors, such as using food to cope by overeating or binge eating, using drugs or alcohol, self-harming, or even attempting suicide.

Both overcontrollers and undercontrollers have developed unhealthy ways of managing emotions. The main difference between them is that you might not be able to see the emotion with overcontrollers, whereas it's generally quite obvious when undercontrollers are struggling with intense feelings. It's important to note that because we learn these patterns early in life they happen largely outside of our conscious awareness, and they tend to stick with us until we recognize them and work to do things differently.

Do you identify with either of these categories? You might see yourself in both, vacillating between these two states; however, when people struggle with emotions, they tend to default to one style or the other. If you're not sure, think about how others would describe you. If you're more overcontrolled, people might say you're "closed off," "cold," "guarded," or "difficult to get to know." If you tend to be undercontrolled, perhaps you've been called a "drama queen" or "drama king" or been told that you "overreact." "Loose cannon" and "unpredictable" are other words that might resonate for you. We'll look more closely at some of the problematic ways of coping in the following chapters. For now, it's helpful for you to be considering, in broad strokes, the potentially unhealthy or even destructive ways you manage your emotions.

Why Do You Struggle with Emotions?

You might wonder why you struggle to manage your emotions effectively at times. Believe it or not, there's a lot we still don't understand about emotions and how the human brain works. But in dialectical behavior therapy, or DBT (More on this shortly!), the biosocial theory explains why people struggle with emotion dysregulation. First, some people are born with a higher level of emotional sensitivity than others. Does this sound familiar? Do you tend to feel things more often and more intensely than others? People with this emotional sensitivity get stuck in intense emotional reactions longer than those who are not as sensitive; so, while those around you seem to "get over" their initial reactions to situations fairly quickly, you might remain stuck there. And, as a more sensitive person, you tend to carry more (both quantity and degree of) painful emotions—anger, sadness, fear, shame, or other difficult feelings—with you on a regular basis.

If this sounds like you, rest assured that you've done nothing to cause this! According to research by Dr. Elaine Aron (2016, xxv), up to 20 percent of the population comprises highly sensitive people. And the cause for this high sensitivity can be genetic: it may be related to a mental health condition you were born with, or it may have been related to problems your mom had while she was pregnant. (No, we're not blaming your mom! But if she had a physical or mental health problem, or if she went through a traumatic or highly stressful situation while she was pregnant with you, it could have affected your development, creating your more highly sensitive temperament.)

It's also important for you to know that being more sensitive isn't all bad (although I know it may feel that way!). While being a highly sensitive person (HSP) might create more pain for you at times, the more sensitive people of the world are usually the more creative and passionate people. You'll likely find that you tend to form more intense connections with others because of your ability to feel things so deeply, as well as to empathize with others. As with so many things, learning to live with your sensitivity comes down to understanding your own emotional reactions and learning to work with them, rather than struggling against them.

This is just the first part of the biosocial theory that helps us to understand why people struggle with emotion dysregulation. The second part is the environment you grew up in. You probably know that our environment plays a large role in our development, and for people who experience emotion dysregulation, trauma has been a common experience—that is, they've been physically, emotionally, verbally, or sexually abused or neglected in some way. That said, having experienced these types of abuse is not a prerequisite to experiencing emotion dysregulation. In DBT, we believe that the combination of an HSP growing up in a *pervasively invalidating environment* (where they received the message that their internal experiences—emotions, thoughts, and physical sensations—were wrong or invalid) results in that person not learning skills to effectively manage emotions. Their environment may also have been abusive or neglectful, but it didn't have to be in order for emotion dysregulation to develop.

Take the example of an HSP growing up in a family of people who are not highly sensitive. It's often difficult for people without high sensitivity to understand the experience of the HSP, which can lead to invalidation, even when it's not intended. For example, people in your family may have asked you things like "Why are you so anxious all the time?" While they were likely trying to understand your experience, their struggle to do so may have caused you to feel like there's something "wrong" with you, or that you shouldn't feel a certain way. Or perhaps you grew up in a family with someone who struggled with a mental illness or addiction or had a serious physical health problem. There may have been little energy left to meet your higher emotional needs.

While no one grows up in a world where their emotions and other internal experiences are always understood and accepted, some people grow up in environments where they regularly receive the message that there's something wrong with them. If you are highly sensitive, and your family was unable to meet your emotional needs, the takeaway here is that it's not your fault that you didn't learn healthy ways of regulating emotions.

Hearing all this, you might find yourself feeling stuck, blaming yourself or your family. I want to emphasize that it's not your fault (quite often it's not your family's fault either) that the emotions you feel sometimes overwhelm you. And, yes, it's still up to you to learn the skills to help you manage your emotions and make things better for yourself! One of the goals in DBT is to move away from black-and-white thinking to find a more balanced perspective. Let's look now at DBT, the treatment that I use in this book that's going to help you do just that.

What Is Dialectical Behavior Therapy and How Will It Help You?

This book is based on a psychological treatment called "dialectical behavior therapy" (DBT), created by Dr. Marsha Linehan, a psychologist in Seattle. She developed it to treat people with borderline personality disorder (BPD), an illness of which one of the main components is this emotion dysregulation I've been talking about. However, since its creation, countless studies have shown how effective DBT skills are in helping people regulate their emotions in healthier ways, even when they don't have BPD. The fact is, DBT is a wonderfully helpful therapy that teaches us skills to manage emotions more effectively. And since life isn't always peaches and roses, we all need skills like these at times. DBT skills are generally broken down into four sets: mindfulness, emotion regulation, distress tolerance, and interpersonal effectiveness. That said, you needn't worry about what type of skill you're using at any given time. What's important is that you use the ones that work for you when you need them!

Because the focus of this book is, first and foremost, helping you to find quick relief from emotions that are hijacking you, when the feelings take over and make it difficult to respond to situations in the ways you might prefer, we're going to look at distress tolerance skills first. These skills will help you get through crisis situations without making things worse by falling back on problematic behaviors you used in the past—things like obsessive thinking, lashing out at others, self-harm, thinking about or engaging in suicidal behaviors, or otherwise acting impulsively or in ways that have negative consequences. Throughout this book, though, you'll find fast-acting, effective, and scientifically proven strategies that will help you stop making problematic choices in the moments when your emotions are intensifying.

But once the immediate crisis is over, you're going to need skills that will help you stop yourself from being hijacked by emotions in the first place. So, you're also going to learn about emotions—importantly, that they all serve a purpose and that we need them. In fact, we can't survive without them! You'll learn that you don't want to shoot these messengers, but instead listen to them. This is where the other DBT skills come in: mindfulness skills will help you get to know yourself better and choose how you want to respond to your emotions effectively. Emotion regulation skills will teach you important information about emotions that will improve your ability to manage painful feelings and increase pleasurable emotions in your life. And interpersonal effectiveness skills will help you to develop healthier relationships with others. In summary, we'll be looking at skills to help you manage difficult or distressing emotions in healthier ways to reduce your pain, increase your pleasurable emotions, and improve your overall quality of life.

While of course skills never come with guarantees, let me reiterate that there have been countless studies showing how helpful DBT is for people who struggle with emotions in the ways I've just described. I've been using this treatment in my practice (and in my own life!) since I started working with people with mental health problems in 2004, and I can tell you that, in my experience, if you put the effort into learning and practicing these skills, you will see some positive changes—even if they start out small.

By the way, you may also find that you don't need each and every skill I'll be presenting in this workbook. Some people are drawn to books like these not because they have a mental health problem, but because they're looking for ways to optimize the skills they already have. If this is you, I believe you'll also find what you're looking for here, and you can pick and choose the skills that fit you best.

Of course, regardless of why you're here, using a skill once or twice won't be very helpful in the long run; the idea with any book like this (and any skills-based psychotherapy) is that you learn skills, and then you make the practice of these skills part of your lifestyle. You may also find, depending on your level of distress, that you need someone to help you learn these skills. If that's the case, don't judge yourself. This isn't always easy work (In fact, it's usually hard!), and unfortunately emotion dysregulation can sometimes prevent people from learning or generalizing skills in different areas of their lives. If this is the case for you, please find someone to support you in your work—a therapist, friend, family member, mentor, and so forth.

When I start working with people, they're often exhausted from putting so much energy into trying to manage their emotions. I get it. But please hang in there. I've seen time and again how these skills can be life changing, and I believe you can learn to manage the emotions you feel—even in those moments when they are intense and your life seems overwhelming—and thrive.

CHAPTER 1

Quick Skills to Reregulate

When it comes to dealing with strong emotions, our first task is to help you stop making things more difficult for yourself. The first step in doing so is to identify the behaviors you turn to that may be creating more chaos in your life. We'll do this in the first part of this chapter, as well as look at skills to help you manage your emotions more effectively without turning to those problematic behaviors. In the second part of the chapter, you'll learn skills that will provide relief from the intense emotions that have you struggling to stay in control or to get back in control.

Target Behaviors

When people struggle with emotions, they often turn to what I refer to as "target behaviors"—behaviors that create problems in the long run, although they might seem helpful in dealing with difficult situations and emotions in the short term. It can be helpful to know that when we're feeling painful emotions, most of us have times when we do things we later regret.

To help you consider what behaviors might be problematic in your life and that you might want to work on, check off those in the following list that you've engaged in over the last three months *in an attempt to manage your emotions* (for example, to help you avoid or escape painful feelings).

- ☐ Lashing out at others

- ☐ Ruminating (dwelling, or rehashing)

- ☐ Engaging in obsessive thinking

- ☐ Procrastinating

- ☐ Seeking reassurance (for example, seeking reassurance from your partner that they love you, or that things will "be all right")

- [ ] Drinking alcohol

- [ ] Using drugs (prescribed, over the counter, or illicit)

- [ ] Lying

- [ ] Gambling

- [ ] Spending money

- [ ] Engaging in repetitive behaviors (such as washing your hands, checking to make sure you've locked the door, counting things)

- [ ] Having sex

- [ ] Watching pornography

- [ ] Catastrophizing (focusing on the worst possible outcome in a situation)

- [ ] Bingeing on food

- [ ] Restricting food

- [ ] Purging food (for example, by vomiting, using laxatives or diuretics)

- [ ] Exercising

- [ ] Shoplifting

- [ ] Video-gaming

- [ ] Surfing the net

- [ ] Using social media

- [ ] Playing games on your phone or tablet

- [ ] Driving recklessly

- [ ] Sleeping

- [ ] Excessively engaging in spiritual practices

- [ ] Watching TV

- [ ] Working

☐ Cleaning

☐ Verbal aggression (yelling or screaming)

☐ Physical aggression (such as hitting or pushing others, throwing things)

☐ Hurting yourself on purpose (for example, cutting, scratching, or burning yourself, or interfering with wound healing)

☐ Thinking about, talking about, or planning suicide

☐ Other: _____

☐ Other: _____

Some of these behaviors, of course, aren't inherently unhealthy, but they can become problematic when you use them excessively, or when you turn to them to avoid uncomfortable or distressing experiences (like emotions). For example, having a spiritual practice you engage in can be very healthy, but if you start using that practice to avoid uncomfortable feelings, or to get your mind off distressing thoughts rather than productively addressing those thoughts, it can become problematic.

With that in mind, think of a recent time you engaged in one of these behaviors to distract yourself from emotions you didn't want to feel. Describe the situation and your behavior. What was the outcome? Did the behavior help? Did it have negative consequences? You may have noticed both.

_____

_____

_____

It's not uncommon for people to turn to unhealthy ways of coping when struggling with intense emotions—for instance, when dealing with stress at work or at home, problems in a relationship, worries about the future, and so forth. Problems occur when you don't have awareness of these behaviors and continue to do them. Not only can your behavior have negative consequences for you and those around you, but in the long run the same behaviors that might provide short-term relief will typically generate more painful emotions, such as guilt, shame, or disappointment in yourself. So be sure to take an honest look at yourself and your behaviors, since having awareness is the first step in making changes. You can also have conversations with people whom you trust and who care about you. These people may have already told you what they think you need to change, but if they haven't, getting an objective perspective from them can be helpful.

Now let's look at the basics of the stress response to help you understand why certain skills you'll learn will provide fast relief from your emotions, hopefully preventing you from engaging these behaviors—making things more difficult for yourself—when emotions start to intensify.

How Stress Dysregulates You

As you'll learn in more depth in chapter 4, an emotion is a *full system response* (Linehan 1993), meaning it's much more than just the way we feel; there's also what we think and what happens in our body when an emotion arises. Let me tell you a tiny bit about the human body's autonomic nervous system (ANS), which regulates our unconscious actions. The ANS consists of two systems. The sympathetic nervous system (SNS) kicks in when we're feeling anxious and is probably best known for the *fight-or-flight response*, which readies the body for action, particularly in situations that threaten our survival (or even perceived threats). Then there's the parasympathetic nervous system (PNS), also known as the *rest and digest* system, which is the counterpart of the SNS. It's the part of our ANS that slows our heart rate and breathing and increases digestion.

Because only one of these systems can be active at a given time, we can learn to intentionally turn on our PNS, which can move us out of an SNS response and help us to slow down and feel calmer. What this means is that when we start to feel an emotion becoming more intense, sometimes we can prevent the escalation of that emotion (or bring it back down) by changing our body's state from SNS activation to PNS activation.

In that spirit, here are some strategies that will quickly help you feel more emotionally balanced. When first learning these skills, it's usually most helpful to practice them before you're emotionally dysregulated, so you know how to do them and what to expect when you are dysregulated. Once you have a handle on them, you can use them when emotions start to intensify. (Here's a tip, though: while these skills will still help when you're already in full-blown crisis mode, if you can catch yourself as emotions start to escalate, before you get really dysregulated, they'll be even more effective.) These skills can help reduce many emotions, including anger, anxiety, shame, and sadness.

Activate Your Parasympathetic Nervous System

The first skills we'll look at, called "reregulating skills," work quickly by activating our PNS. In moments when painful emotions are intensifying and our SNS is activated, we can consciously turn our PNS on to get our body back to a state of equilibrium.

The forward bend. This is my favorite reregulating skill! Bend over as though you're trying to touch your toes, take some slow, deep breaths, and hang out there for thirty to sixty seconds if you can.

When you're ready, stand up again—slowly, so you don't fall over! It doesn't matter if you can actually touch your toes, and you can also do this sitting down if you need to by sticking your head between your knees. The key here is getting your head below your heart.

Focus on your exhale. It may sound cliché, but breathing is truly one of the best ways to calm intense emotions. This skill is another of my favorites. As you inhale, count in your head. As you exhale, count at the same pace, making sure your exhale is at least a little bit longer than your inhale. For example, if you get to four when you inhale, make sure you exhale to at least five. Focusing on making your exhale longer than your inhale activates the PNS. By the way, pairing this exercise with the forward bend is a double whammy to problematic emotions, so while doing a forward bend, focus on making your exhale longer than your inhale as best as you can.

Suck on lemons! Okay, so maybe don't actually go that far, but sucking on a tart candy or eating something tart like salt-and-vinegar chips—or even imagining that you are (Did your mouth just start to water?!)—stimulates the salivary glands, which are connected to our PNS (through another handy-dandy part of our body known as the "vagus nerve," for those science nerds in the audience). The long and short of it is that producing more saliva moves our body into that rest and digest PNS mode, helping us feel calmer and come back down from that fight-or-flight state.

More Skills for Quickly Regulating Emotions

There are other ways of activating your PNS that we'll go over later. For now, we're going to stick with skills that work fast. Now we're going to look at other skills for getting relief from intense emotions; these don't involve activating the PNS. Be sure to try all of these techniques (more than once!) in order to find what works best for you.

Activate your dive reflex. Putting your face in cold water, activating the mammalian dive reflex, is another technique that can help you quickly break out of a crisis cycle and get your emotions reregulated (Linehan 2014). All mammals have this reflex; since we can't breathe under water, our body conserves oxygen by slowing down the heart. The good news for us humans is that this reflex can also help us to regulate our emotions—fast!

First, it's important to know that if you have a heart problem (including low blood pressure), are taking medications called "beta blockers," or have disordered eating (restricting or purging), you can't do this skill, so stop reading here! If you're not sure whether you can do this skill safely, check with your doctor before reading any further, because this skill can actually cause you to pass out. If you're 100 percent certain that these caveats do not apply to you, go to the nearest sink, fill it with the coldest water possible, and put your face in the water for thirty seconds (or as long as you can). If you're fearful of trying this technique, alternatively you can splash cold water on your face or hold an ice pack over your eyes, but to activate the dive reflex, it works best if you hold your breath and tip yourself forward to trick your body into thinking you're in water.

If you're not able to use this skill for whatever reason, keep in mind you can still use temperature to help you manage emotions: whenever the body is required to adjust to cold temperatures, the SNS system turns off and the PNS is activated. This means that holding a cold compress or ice pack to your forehead, your wrists, or the back of your neck, for instance, will still help. Or, if you live in a colder climate, getting yourself outside for a walk in the winter might do the trick as well!

Intense exercise. Most people know that there's an association between aerobic exercise and emotional well-being, but the nature of this link is still not well understood (Bernstein and McNally 2017). (Yes, this is yet another thing about our human brain that we still have a lot to learn about.) We do know for certain that intense exercise boosts certain chemicals in our brain, reducing emotional pain and improving our mood and our ability to manage emotions. Here's what this connection boils down to: if you're stressed out and emotions are beginning to overwhelm you, do some jumping jacks or lunges in your bedroom, go for a run around the block, or run up and down your stairs. As with the other skills in this section, doing so will help interrupt a cycle of feelings, thoughts, and behaviors that might otherwise take over, opening space for you to respond to what you're feeling in a healthier, more adaptive way.

These two techniques, and those for activating the PNS, are all short-term methods for regulating your emotions. They can create an opportunity for you to get yourself unhijacked from your emotions temporarily, so that you can think more clearly about what you can do to not make a situation worse by falling back into old patterns. Once you're unhijacked, it's time to make changes. Before we cover that topic, it can be helpful to take a good, hard look at what you're ready to commit to changing, so let's first look at the pros and cons of changing your behavior.

The Pros and Cons of Change

While you might be new to the idea of managing emotions in healthier ways, some of you have likely been here before: perhaps you've done the self-help thing, or you've even tried therapy, and yet here you are, still struggling. Or maybe you've been dealing with emotion dysregulation for so long you're not sure you can actually change at this point. There might be other beliefs getting in your way as well, preventing you from feeling fully committed to doing this work. And yet at least a part of you likely believes there's a possibility that this book might help, otherwise I don't think you'd still be reading.

If you find yourself on the fence about whether or not change is possible for you, it's important to take an open, honest look at that ambivalence. It can take a lot of energy and effort to make the kinds of changes we'll be talking about, and you won't get very far if you're not truly committed. So, to help you decide if you're ready and willing to do this work, let's look at the pros and cons of changing behavior (Linehan 2014). If you find that you're really *not* ready to do a specific piece of work yet (like eliminating your use of cannabis or alcohol), the good news is that you're probably going to be able to find a way to change some of the unhealthy patterns you've developed in your life (like eliminating use of harder drugs); you can always work your way back to the more challenging behaviors later.

In DBT we do a four-column pros and cons chart rather than the traditional two columns. Four columns help us look at the situation from all sides, exploring the pros and cons of changing and of not changing our behavior. This format often provides new perspectives and insights. First, have a look at this sample chart.

Pros of Changing Behavior	Cons of Changing Behavior
Increase my quality of life (3/3).	It will be hard work (2/3).
Improve relationships with my partner and my friends (3/3).	Pushes me out of my comfort zone (1/3).
Changing my behavior might help me keep my job (2/3).	I'm afraid I won't be able to do it (2/3).
Feel better about myself (3/3).	It's an admission that there's something wrong (1/3).
Reduce my feelings of guilt and shame (3/3).	People might have higher expectations of me if I'm coping better (2/3).
Total: 14	Total: 8
Pros of *Not* Changing Behavior	**Cons of *Not* Changing Behavior**
I don't have to challenge myself (2/3).	Things will stay the same (2/3).
Things will stay the same; it's comfortable (2/3).	It will be harder to reach my goals (3/3).
Total: 4	I'll continue to damage my relationships (3/3).
	I might do more damage to myself as time goes on (3/3).
	I'll continue to feel bad about myself (2/3).
	Total: 13

Now it's your turn. In the blank chart provided, fill in your own thoughts about changing your behavior. You can refer back to the responses in the sample chart if you get stuck. Remember to think short term as well as long term, considering how your choices now might affect you, your goals, and your relationships with others over the short and long terms. Do your best to let yourself brainstorm. If some responses overlap, don't worry; just write them down as they come to you. It makes sense for there to be repetition (for example, some of the pros of changing behavior may be the same as the cons of not changing). Finally, it will be helpful for you to come back to this exercise at different times to help you consider different perspectives: brainstorm right now, and in a couple of days come back to look at what you've written. You might also return to review this chart as you continue to learn more about yourself, your target behavior, and the skills that will help you make changes. You can download additional copies of this form, as well as other worksheets for this book, at this book's website: http://www.newharbinger.com/49647. (See the very back of this book for more details.)

Pros and Cons Chart

Pros of Changing Behavior	Cons of Changing Behavior
Pros of *Not* Changing Behavior	Cons of *Not* Changing Behavior

Depending on your readiness to change, you might find that you have more responses in favor of not changing behavior than in favor of changing behavior; if you take a closer look, however, you might find that some of your responses are more important than others. To help determine this, rate each of your responses from 1 (not that important) to 3 (highly important), and then add up each category, as I did in the sample chart. Chances are this will create a more accurate picture for you of what's truly important.

How did that go? Take a minute to reflect on this exercise by answering the following questions.

Were you able to identify factors that are motivating you to change your behavior? If so, what stood out most?

_____

_____

_____

Were you able to identify factors that are preventing you from making these changes? What's keeping you stuck?

_____

_____

_____

Based on the Pros and Cons Chart you filled out, are you able to set a goal for yourself around making changes? For instance, maybe you're able to fully commit to learning skills to help you manage emotions in healthier ways, or perhaps you're willing to let go of certain unhealthy or self-destructive things you've been doing, but there are other behaviors you're not willing to change yet. Write your goal(s) here:

_____

_____

_____

If you're not yet able to come up with a goal, that's okay! There are a few things you can still do to help yourself get there. First, you might continue to read this workbook and practice the skills you're learning until you feel more ready. Part of you might be reluctant to make changes, even though another part knows this is the way to go. If this sentiment resonates, just give yourself some time. Continue reading this book, and you might start to feel more ready to dip your toe in. Practicing the skills you'll be learning in this book will also increase your self-awareness, so you'll become more aware of the choices you're making and the behaviors you're engaging in that are doing you more harm than good.

If you're stuck in a place of uncertainty right now, move on to chapter 3 to start learning skills to help increase your self-awareness. You can then return to this section when you have a better idea of what you'd like to work on. If you've managed to set a goal of changing a behavior, the next step is to get to know that behavior better by doing a behavioral analysis.

Behavioral Analysis

Hopefully you've already started using some of the skills you've learned in this book, but in order to make meaningful and lasting changes you need to have a good understanding of why a target behavior is happening in the first place. What purpose has the behavior been serving for you? What other factors contribute to the likelihood of you doing the behavior? What triggers it? The following behavioral analysis (BA) will help increase your understanding of the behavior so you'll be in a better position to work on changing it (with all of the skills to come!). First, have a look at the sample BA completed by Charlie, who would like to stop eating emotionally.

Behavioral Analysis

Date filled out: Saturday, Dec. 12, 2020   Date of target behavior: Friday, December 11, 2020

What *target behavior* am I analyzing? I "ate my feelings:" I overate after dinner on Friday night, eating about half a big bag of chips, then half a big bag of M&M's, and four chocolate chip cookies.
What things in myself and my environment made me *vulnerable* to engaging in the target behavior? (What on that day made it more likely that I would engage in the target behavior?) • I was stressed after a difficult week at work. • I had a lot of unstructured time, as I had half a day off work. • I skipped the hike with the dogs I had planned because I didn't feel like it. • I had bought some junk food I shouldn't keep in the house because I know I can't resist!
What prompting event *in the environment* started me on the chain to the target behavior? Mom left me a message telling me she missed me, and I felt guilty because I've been limiting my contact with my family.
What are the *links* in the chain between the prompting event and the target behavior? (Be very specific and detailed about what happened between the prompting event and the target behavior.) • Friday afternoon I got a voicemail from Mom telling me she missed me and asking me to call her. • I've been limiting my contact with my parents because I know it's not a healthy relationship, but I felt guilty right away. • I thought about what a bad person I am. • Then I felt angry at Mom for guilting me. • I judged myself for being angry at her, and then I felt angry with myself. • I felt overwhelmed with all of these emotions. • Why does this keep happening over and over? I should be able to manage in healthier ways by now! • I just wanted to escape and isolate myself. • I had an urge to eat and thought that it would make me feel better. • I grabbed my laptop and the bag of chips and headed to my room where I started to eat while watching Netflix. • Once the chips were gone, I went back to the kitchen to get the M&M's and the cookies and took them back to my room to keep eating.

Keeping in mind that consequences can be immediate or delayed, answer the following questions about your behavior:

1. What were the *negative consequences?*

- I was so full I was uncomfortable.
- I felt shame for doing this again.
- I didn't even enjoy the food.
- It cost a lot of money.
- I'm not working toward my goal of getting physically healthier.

2. What were the *positive consequences?*

- It felt good in the moment.
- It distracted me from thoughts of Mom and Dad.
- It's easy and comfortable.

While you probably have at least some insight into your target behavior already, you might be surprised by what you learn about your behavior when you analyze it this way. If you've identified more than one target behavior, choose one to start with, and complete four to five BAs on that behavior. Once you've made significant progress in eliminating that behavior, you can start with the next one. Here's a blank form for you to use (you can download copies of it at this book's website: http://www.newharbinger.com/49647).

Behavioral Analysis

Date filled out: _____   Date of target behavior: _____

What *target behavior* am I analyzing?
What things in myself and my environment made me *vulnerable* to engaging in the target behavior? (What on that day made it more likely that I would engage in the target behavior?)
What prompting event *in the environment* started me on the chain to the target behavior?
What are the *links* in the chain between the prompting event and the target behavior? (Be very specific and detailed about what happened between the prompting event and the target behavior.)

Keeping in mind that consequences can be immediate or delayed, answer the following questions about your behavior:

1. What were the *negative consequences?*

2. What were the *positive consequences?*

Once you've completed four to five BAs on your first target behavior, review what you've written, and answer the following questions.

Are there specific things that seem to make you more vulnerable to engaging in this behavior? (What made it more likely for you to engage in the behavior on that day? In the sample BA, for example, having unstructured time increased Charlie's vulnerability. Other vulnerability factors could be not getting enough sleep or dealing with a lot of stress). List any you can think of here.

_____

_____

Are there themes to the events that prompt the target behavior? (For example, is the behavior usually linked to a specific situation—perhaps at work or in a relationship—or a certain person?)

_____

_____

Looking at the links in the chain, do you notice themes, perhaps thoughts that you know are unrealistic or self-judgmental (such as _I'm a bad person_)? Often people notice that certain painful emotions (like anger or shame) contribute to target behaviors. Write any thoughts here.

_____

_____

Although you've already considered the pros and cons of your behavior generally, looking at specific instances of the behavior can sometimes provide new information. Reviewing the BAs, see if you can dig deeper into the pros and cons of this behavior.

Positive consequences: _____

_____

Negative consequences: _____

_____

The most common reason for a lack of progress in eliminating a target behavior is that we don't have a thorough understanding of the behavior (Linehan 1993). So, when you're completing a BA, remember that sometimes the devil is in the details!

The BA can be a difficult process since it's not usually much fun to really think about something you did that you're now regretting, and sometimes people feel shame, anger, or disappointment in themselves while filling out BAs. Think of this as short-term pain for long-term gain, because until you have a good understanding of why you're doing a particular behavior, it's going to be hard for you to change the behavior and stick to those changes in the long run. And remember, you won't be doing BAs forever! It might also help you to know that the BA can play another role in helping you to stop the behavior: if you remind yourself of the paperwork you have to fill out when you do the target behavior, you might find yourself not so eager to act on that urge!

Wrapping Up

In this chapter you learned a number of skills to help you regulate your emotions when things start to get out of control. You also started getting a better idea of what *out of control* looks like for you, and what behaviors you'd like to change to help you lead an emotionally healthier life. And you've (hopefully!) already taken the first step to making healthy changes by learning more about these behaviors through the Pros and Cons Chart and the Behavioral Analysis.

Developing awareness, learning new ways of living your life, and making changes typically take a lot of time and energy, so don't be discouraged if you're not seeing the results you'd like just yet! In the next chapter, we're going to work on skills some more to help you avoid falling back into those problematic behaviors. For now, you've got lots of work to do, so hang in there, and be sure to put what you're learning into practice as we go.

CHAPTER 2

Learning to Tolerate Distress

So far, we've looked at some of the problematic behaviors you turn to when difficult emotions hijack you, and you've learned a number of skills to help you get fast relief from those emotions by changing your body's chemistry. Hopefully you've been considering those behaviors and their consequences through the Pros and Cons Chart, and learning more about them through the Behavioral Analysis.

In this chapter we're going to continue looking at skills, in the form of distress tolerance skills, that will provide you with quick relief from painful emotions. These skills will help you act differently in the heat of the moment by changing your thinking. In contrast to the skills you learned in the last chapter, these might be a bit harder to use until you get familiar with them, but in the long run they'll provide you with more flexibility in managing your emotions. Then we'll look at putting these skills together to help you manage urges, whether it's to stuff your feelings, lash out at others, drink or use drugs, or engage in any of the other target behaviors we looked at in the last chapter.

RESISTTing the Urge

Although it's often difficult for people to change target behaviors, especially when they've been a habit for a long time, there are lots of techniques you can use to help yourself not act on urges. In DBT these are known as *distress tolerance skills* (Linehan 2014) because they help us learn to tolerate the distress we're experiencing and resist the urge to avoid it through unhealthy behaviors. Let's take a look at these skills using the acronym RESISTT (Van Dijk 2013):

R: Reframe.

E: Engage in an activity mindfully.

S: Do something for someone else.

I: Experience *intense* sensations.

S: Shut it out.

T: Think neutral thoughts.

T: Take a break.

As you're reading about these skills, it will be important for you to make a personalized list for yourself of all the skills you can use when painful emotions start to intensify and you notice an urge arising. You'll refer back to this distress tolerance skills list as we go.

R: Reframe. We can learn to manage emotions more effectively by *reframing*, or changing, our perspective about something. You might be familiar with the sayings "making lemonade out of lemons" and "finding the silver lining in a situation;" both are examples of reframing—finding a positive in what seems to be negative—making problematic stuff more bearable. There are many ways to reframe; here are a few techniques for you to try:

- You can compare yourself to someone else who isn't coping as well as you are. This isn't about minimizing your problems, nor is it about putting the other person down. Rather, it's about helping you see that even though things are difficult for you right now, they could also be worse (for example, "Things are hard right now, but my friend Kelly is in the hospital, so I can also see that things could be worse").

- You can compare yourself now to a time in your life when you weren't coping as well (for example, "I'm really struggling right now, but this time last year I was still smoking weed to cope").

- Or you could compare your own situation to a broader situation in the world (for example, "Things are hard for me since I lost my job, but I'm grateful I have my family to help me through these difficult times, whereas others might not have this kind of support").

As you consider how you might think differently about your situation, keep in mind that reframing does *not* mean minimizing your pain or telling yourself you should "suck it up;" it's about trying to see another perspective. For example, if you try to reframe by comparing yourself to others, you're not saying, "Those people have it way worse than I do, I should be able to just get over this." It's important to acknowledge the pain you're dealing with, and then work on changing your perspective.

The way we talk to ourselves about what's happening in our lives can also change the way we think and feel about things. And unfortunately, it's a fairly common human experience to focus on the negative, or *catastrophize*. Changing your negative thoughts about a situation usually makes it more tolerable, and you'll be more likely to get through it without doing things that could make it worse.

To help change your negative self-talk, write out some coping statements to use when you get into situations that trigger intense emotions. That way you'll be less likely to make the situation worse, and more likely to cope in effective ways instead of turning to target behaviors. Here are some examples of coping statements:

- *These feelings are painful, but I know I can bear them.*

- *I can get through this.*

- *This pain will not last forever.*

If you can't think of more encouraging or neutral ways of talking to yourself, feel free to use the examples I provided, if they resonate for you, or ask someone who supports you for help. You can also ask yourself what you would say to a loved one if they were in your shoes. We'll be doing more work on this later in this workbook as well, so don't worry if you're struggling.

How can you reframe to help yourself when things get difficult? Add your ideas to your distress tolerance skills list.

E: Engage in an activity. Getting your mind off a difficult situation and the emotions associated with it is also usually helpful for regulating emotions. Researchers (Koole 2009) have found that instructing someone to not think about a painful, unwanted emotion increases that emotion, whereas telling someone to think about something specific in place of that emotion greatly increases the person's ability to not think about it. The important lesson here is that if you don't want to think about or feel something, trying to not have that experience is pretty much going to guarantee that you'll have it. And rather than wrestling with something you don't want to experience in a deliberate attempt to stop feeling what you feel, it's better to develop the capacity to let the things that bother you be there as you turn your attention to some other activity.

There's a subtle but critical difference between trying to push an experience away, ignoring or avoiding it, and turning your mind to something else. Christopher Germer (2009) notes that when you try to push something away, it goes into the basement and lifts weights! Not only does that thought or feeling not go away (although it may seem like it does at times), it's actually just in hiding and often comes back stronger. Instead, if you turn your mind to something else, you're acknowledging the difficult experience and then moving your attention elsewhere, without judgment. (If you're familiar with mindfulness, by the way, this may sound familiar, but we'll explore that topic in the next chapter.)

When you're in crisis, you want to be able to distract yourself with activities that will hold your attention. You probably do this already, at least to a certain extent. Think of things you do naturally when you're getting emotional about something and you're trying to not let your emotions escalate. Do you go for a walk? Listen to music? Call a friend? List some of the activities you do to help get your mind off the problem.

_____   _____

_____   _____

_____   _____

The list of activities you could come up with is pretty much endless, so thinking about what you do already when things get difficult is a good starting point. Add these to your list of distress tolerance skills, and then keep brainstorming about what else you could do that you don't already do. The goal is for your list to be as long as possible so that when you find your emotions intensifying, you have many options for activities to help take your mind off the situation.

S: Do something for someone else. Sometimes, doing something for someone else is an effective way to get our mind off a problem: perhaps visiting a friend who can't get out of the house, cooking your partner their favorite meal, or crafting with your neighbors' kids. What ideas can you come up with? Add them to your distress tolerance skills list.

I: Experience intense sensations. Generating intense physical sensations can sometimes distract us from painful emotions. What physical sensations might take your mind off your emotions? For example, if you turn to self-harm to deal with painful emotions, Marsha Linehan suggests holding an ice cube in your hand (2003b); this causes an intense sensation but doesn't come with the negative consequences of self-harm. Here are some other things you might try:

- Take a hot or cold bath or shower (Keep in mind that the cold water, if you can go that route, will also help by activating your PNS!), or go for a walk in cold or hot weather.

- Snap a rubber band on your wrist.

- Chew on crushed ice or frozen fruit.

Think about what activities you can try to help you get through a crisis, and add them to your distress tolerance skills list.

S: Shut it out. Quite often, physically leaving a situation and going somewhere calm and quiet will make it more likely that you can use your skills and manage emotions more effectively. Sometimes, of course, this isn't enough, and you may find yourself continuing to dwell on the problem even after you've physically left the situation. This is when shutting it out—the DBT skill known as *pushing away* (Linehan 2014)—can be helpful. With this skill, you use your imagination to convince your mind that the problem isn't something that can be worked on now, and that it needs to be put away for the time being.

The first step to shutting it out is to write out the problem (or list of problems, if there's more than one) contributing to your emotional pain. Next, ask yourself if this is a problem you can solve *right now*: Do you have the skills to solve the problem? Is there a solution to the problem that you can start working on in this very moment? If you see that you can solve the problem, then stop right here and solve it! Shutting it out is only effective if you can convince your mind that you can't do anything about the current problem right now.

For a problem you can't solve, close your eyes and get a sense of something that represents it. For example, if you had an argument with your boss, you might conjure an image of your boss, or visualize their name. (If you can't visualize very well, see if you can get a *sense* of the problem in some way, or *feel* it.) Next, imagine yourself placing that representation of your problem in a box, putting a lid on the box, and tying the lid on with string or rope—or chains! The goal here is to convince your mind that the problem can't be worked on now and must be put away for the time being, so do what you have to do to shut it out. For example, you might need to imagine putting the box on a shelf in a closet, shutting the closet door, and putting a padlock on the door.

You can also make this technique more concrete: take the problem you've written down on a piece of paper and literally put it away; tell a *worry doll* (a doll that is put under the pillow, which will take over the worrying for the person, allowing them to sleep better rather than lying awake worrying) about the problem before you go to sleep at night to alleviate your anxiety about the problem; or put the problem in a "God box," a container with an opening on top. When using a God box, you write your problem, worry, or difficult decision on a piece of paper and put it in the box, turning the matter over to God (or "higher power," or whatever version of this that fits for you).

If you shut the problem out in some way already, fantastic; add your method to your distress tolerance skills list. If this concept is new to you, write out some ideas you'd be willing to try. Keep in mind that this skill, and any other approach that involves avoiding thinking certain thoughts or feelings, can be helpful for some people, but pushing thoughts and emotions away often makes them stronger, so this skill should be used sparingly.

T: Think neutral thoughts. Focusing your attention on neutral (or positive) thoughts can also distract you from emotions and urges, thereby reducing their intensity. These neutral thoughts can be anything that distract you from painful thoughts and emotions; for example, one of my favorite superheroes recites the street names, in order, of the neighborhood they grew up in. Here are some examples of thinking neutral thoughts:

- Count (for example, count your inhalations as you do paced breathing, or count backward from 100 by 3s).

- Say a prayer or repeat a mantra that you find comforting, such as "It is what it is" or "Peace and calm."

- Sing your favorite song or recite a nursery rhyme or poem.

Again, you might already be doing something like this. If so, it's important to validate that this is a skillful behavior, and to make a point of using it in a conscious way. What are some neutral things you can think about when you're getting dysregulated? Be sure to add these to your distress tolerance skills list!

T: Take a break. Taking a break in some way when emotions are intense can also help you get through a crisis without making it worse (Linehan 2003a). What might a break look like for you? Are there responsibilities you need to get away from for a short period to clear your head and to help yourself feel less overwhelmed? Maybe you need to skip the errands you had planned and order takeout for dinner tonight so there's no cooking or cleanup to worry about. Get creative in thinking about this technique. Can you take a day off work? If you can't take a whole day away from your responsibilities (work, family, or otherwise), maybe you can go out for lunch or take a short walk to get some fresh air and a change of environment.

Taking a break might also involve practicing mindfulness, relaxation exercises, or imagery techniques that help you feel calmer or more at peace. (We'll be looking at these skills throughout this book, so don't worry if you don't know about them yet!) Just remember that breaks shouldn't be used too often because they, too, can turn into avoidance, interfering with your responsibilities or long-term goals. Be sure to add these ideas to your distress tolerance skills list.

Let's now look at putting all of these skills together in a way that will make it more likely that you'll be able to avoid acting on your urge to engage in target behaviors when painful emotions arise.

Urge Management

The first step in the process of managing an urge is to get your list of distress tolerance skills together. Decide what form your list will take: Are you a traditional paper person? Or are you going to make this list on your laptop, phone, or tablet? Whatever you decide, return to chapter 1 to quickly review the skills we looked at that will help you change your body's chemistry to regulate your emotions. At least one of these skills should go at the top of your list: activating your parasympathetic nervous system (PNS) by doing a forward bend, focusing on your exhale, or sucking on something tart; activating your dive reflex with cold water; or doing intense exercise. You may want to write out some instructions instead of just the name of the skill. We all know how hard it can be to think straight when we're dysregulated, and one of the goals of this list is to make it as easy as possible for you to integrate these skills into your life.

Next, go back to the beginning of this chapter and review the RESISTT skills. Add all of the related skills you came up with to your distress tolerance skills list. Now that you have a list and you're ready for a crisis, here are the steps to follow when you notice an urge arise.

Step 1: Rate the urge from 1 (it's there, but barely noticeable) to 10 (it's super intense).

Step 2: Set an alarm (on your phone, your tablet, the stove, or your alarm clock) for fifteen minutes, and make a commitment to yourself that for the next fifteen minutes you're going to use skills instead of acting on the urge.

Step 3: Pull out your distress tolerance skills list and do the first thing on the list. This is likely going to be one of the skills that changes your body chemistry, and you should be a little more regulated once you've done the skill. Now read what's next on your list. If it's "Call Mom," but it's midnight and you know she's fast asleep, go to the next skill. If it's "Go for a walk" but it's midnight and not safe to walk alone, go on to the next thing. If the next thing on your list is "Do a crossword puzzle," and you're not able to concentrate… You got it, go on to the next thing on your list. This is why you want your list to be as long as possible. A long list will offer you many different options for the many kinds of situations that can contribute to dysregulation. Some skills will be more effective at certain times than others. When you're feeling dysregulated, the important thing is to keep using these skills until the fifteen minutes is up and your timer goes off.

Step 4: When the timer goes off, rerate your urge. Hopefully it's come down and you can pat yourself on the back for a job well done and continue with your day. If the urge has stayed the same or perhaps even increased, then ideally set the timer for another fifteen minutes and go back to using your skills. But even if you don't follow through with using more skills in that particular moment—and let's face it, we probably all have moments when we give in and act on our urges—you should still congratulate yourself for using skills first, instead of just going straight to that target behavior like you normally would have. This is progress. Gradually over time you'll retrain yourself so that you're using more and more skills, rather than immediately acting on the urge. It takes energy and practice to avoid certain behaviors, but as you're hopefully beginning to see, this work will be worth it in the long run.

Rescue Skill: Progressive Muscle Relaxation

Before we wrap up each chapter, I'll leave you with a *rescue skill* that can provide you with quick relief from intense emotions. Progressive muscle relaxation (PMR), the exercise discussed here, is another way to activate the PNS.

When we're in that SNS (sympathetic nervous system) fight-or-flight state, there's a lot of energy pulsing through our body. PMR is one simple (but not easy!) way to activate the rest and digest PNS system to release that energy. In this exercise you'll tense and release each muscle group, starting with your feet and moving upward until you get to your head. (Or, if you prefer, you can go in the opposite direction.) It usually takes some practice outside of difficult situations in order for you to access PMR when you need it.

The following list summarizes the muscle groups you'll focus on during this exercise; you can start on either side of your body or do both sides at once. As you work your way through this list, hold the tension in each muscle group for about five seconds, then release; give yourself about a ten-second break before moving on to the next muscle group. Just be sure you don't squeeze your muscles so hard that you hurt yourself!

1. *Foot:* curl your toes downward, and tense your whole foot.

2. *Lower leg and foot:* flex your foot, pulling your toes toward you.

3. *Legs:* squeeze your thigh muscles while doing step 2.

4. *Hand:* clench your fist.

5. *Arm:* keeping your fist clenched, bring your forearm up toward your shoulder (as if you're showing off your bicep!).

6. *Buttocks:* squeeze them tight!

7. *Stomach:* suck in those abs!

8. *Chest:* take a deep breath.

9. *Neck and shoulders:* raise your shoulders up to your ears.

10. *Mouth:* open your mouth as wide as you can!

11. *Eyes:* squeeze your eyelids shut.

12. *Forehead:* raise your eyebrows as high as they'll go.

If you're more of a visual or aural learner, there are lots of online tutorials that can walk you through this exercise, at least until you get the hang of it. Over time you'll find that you can also take a shortcut if you'd like, tensing and releasing several muscle groups at once instead of doing them separately. Finally, pairing PMR with the paced breathing exercise you learned in the last chapter, making your exhale longer than your inhale, will make it even more effective for managing intense emotions.

Wrapping Up

In this chapter you learned more skills to provide relief when emotions start to intensify. Hopefully you've started keeping a list of these skills to help you manage in those difficult situations. Remember, most of us find it harder to think straight when emotions get intense, so it's important that you don't have to think about what you can do to help yourself in those moments. You want to be able to just pull out your list that can tell you what to do.

As you work your way through this book, please take your time, and be sure you're really absorbing the skills and putting them into practice. You may find that not all the skills work for you or resonate for you, or you may find that you're feeling overwhelmed or not quite ready to do all the work I'm suggesting. If that's the case, don't worry! Just add what works or what you're able to do right now to your repertoire of skills; you can always come back for a refresher later. And if you're really struggling right now, please know that asking for help is a sign of strength, not weakness. Reach out to people who can support you in the work you're doing. You may even find that you need to work through things with a professional. Whatever route you choose, if you stick with it, I'm confident these skills will help you move in a healthier direction, so hang in there.

In the next chapter you'll learn some skills that will help you continue to increase your awareness of yourself and why you do the things you do. So, when you're ready, turn the page.

CHAPTER 3

Getting to Know Yourself with Mindfulness

So far, we've focused on skills that will help you reregulate your emotions when things get difficult, whether it's daily life stresses or a major meltdown about something specific. You've also been learning more about yourself and why you engage in target behaviors at times. In this chapter we'll look at a skill called "mindfulness," which will be helpful in a number of ways.

What Is Mindfulness?

Mindfulness is doing one thing at a time, in the present moment, with your full attention, and with acceptance. Another way of saying this is that mindfulness is intentionally being more aware of the present moment, and not judging whatever you find in that moment. Western philosophers have described it as a means of increasing awareness of self—of thoughts, emotions, and physical sensations. The ancient practice of mindfulness has become popular in the mental health world over the last few decades, and since it's popularization in the Western world starting in the late 1970s, scientists have been studying mindfulness and have discovered all sorts of benefits to this practice, some of which I'll outline here.

Mindfulness enhances our cognitive abilities, including our ability to pay attention and remember things. It also improves our brain's executive functions, including things like learning and retaining new information and using this information to solve problems, as well as accessing information, thinking about and implementing solutions, planning for the future, considering consequences, and making decisions. Researchers have even found evidence that mindfulness may help reduce the effects Alzheimer's disease (Heutz 2017)!

Mindfulness also enhances our physical health. It can improve sleep and reduce fatigue; improve various medical conditions, such as high blood pressure and chronic pain; as well as increase our ability to cope with physical illness. Mindfulness also reduces cortisol (the stress hormone), decreases inflammation, and improves immune function.

Most importantly for the purposes of this workbook, studies have shown that mindfulness can reduce the symptoms of mental health problems, such as depression, anxiety, general psychological stress, and substance abuse, by increasing our self-awareness and our ability to tolerate uncomfortable or distressing experiences (such as emotions, thoughts, and physical sensations). In addition, mindfulness improves our ability to have empathy and compassion for ourselves and others, and it activates a part of our brain that's connected to experiencing happiness and optimism. In other words, it helps us feel good!

Hopefully you're starting to see that mindfulness is helpful in many different ways. Of course, the goal of this workbook is to help you manage your emotions more effectively, so let's take a closer look at how mindfulness helps with this specifically.

How Mindfulness Can Help You Regulate Emotions

Have you noticed yourself spending a lot of time thinking about the past? Have you noticed yourself dwelling on or rehashing something that happened long ago (maybe when you were younger you were bullied, you were a bully, or you lost someone you were close to) or even just yesterday (perhaps a fight with your partner, or something a coworker said that rubbed you the wrong way)? We typically have themes that we rehash over and over again, and in doing so we're often judging events or people in a negative way (for example, thinking that your partner *shouldn't* have said those hurtful things, or that your coworker clearly *doesn't know anything*). See if you can identify any themes in what you tend to dwell on, as well as what emotions come up for you when you're ruminating about and judging events, others, and yourself.

_____

_____

_____

Now, what about the future? Do you get stuck in what-ifs, or catastrophizing? We often create imaginary scenarios that we live in as though they're actually happening (for example, you might worry you'll make a mistake at work that will cost you your job; or after an argument with your partner, you worry they'll leave you), and thinking about these scenarios can cause anxiety and other emotions. Judgments of self and others often come into play as well, adding to the emotions. If this sounds familiar, make some notes here about what future events you tend to imagine happening, and the emotions that arise as a result.

_____

_____

_____

To be clear, many people have lived through traumatic experiences, such as childhood abuse, natural disasters, suicide attempts, or criminal victimization, that are, of course, extremely painful. If you've had experiences like these, however, consider this: When you get stuck in those memories, reliving the event, judging yourself or others, wishing it hadn't happened, and so on, is this helping you in any way? Does thinking about an event over and over help you move on from it? Does continually wondering, for instance, what would have happened if you had done something differently, or what your life would have been like if a particular thing hadn't happened to you, change how you think or feel about your experience?

More than likely the answer is no. In fact, by allowing yourself to stay with this kind of thinking, you usually experience painful emotions that wouldn't otherwise be there. While most people engage in rumination at times, excessive rumination can preoccupy us, taking up excess space in our head and interfering with our ability to live life fully. It can affect our mood, triggering intense painful feelings like shame, anger, anxiety, and sadness.

Mindfulness can help prevent painful emotions from arising by increasing your awareness of when you're stuck in the past or the future, caught up in judgments. And this increased awareness will allow you to change your thinking rather than stay stuck in it.

Hopefully you're starting to see that when you live more in the present moment with acceptance, there's less pain. If, in this moment, you're reading these pages mindfully, what painful emotions come up for you? Probably none. Painful emotions start to arise when you're reading this book and your mind starts to take you into the past or the future. For example, you start to think about things you did in the past that you feel guilt or shame about, or you start to worry that you won't be able to put the skills you're learning into practice and you feel anxious and hopeless. Likewise, if you start to judge, your emotional pain will increase. For example, if you're struggling to understand some of these ideas and you judge yourself as "stupid," or if you judge yourself for needing these skills, you'll likely feel shame, anger, or disappointment in yourself.

Finally, mindfulness can help you choose how to respond to the urges that strong emotions trigger. As we've already discussed, we all have urges at times. Many people learn healthy ways of managing their emotions in childhood, so these kinds of urges might not be a problem; but for some, acting on problematic urges has become a habitual, unhealthy way of dealing with emotional pain.

So how do you start working on taking control of your life? As you read in chapter 1, the first step to changing behavior is to increase your awareness of it. Mindfulness will help you to be more aware of your thoughts, physical sensations, and emotions, so that you'll notice the urges you're experiencing more quickly, giving you the ability (over time) to choose how you want to act in a situation, rather than reacting in your old, habitual way. Gradually, as you practice mindfulness, you'll be more able to resist the urge and choose new, healthier ways of responding.

Mindfulness Helps You Get to Know Yourself

Another benefit of living in the here and now and becoming more aware and accepting of yourself, noticing emotions, physical sensations, and thoughts you're experiencing, is that you'll get to know yourself better. Have you ever had the sense that you don't really know who you are? When someone asks what your values are, what's important to you, or what your goals are, do you struggle to find the answers? This might cause you to feel as though you don't have a good sense of your own identity. Many of us have experienced this to some degree, especially when we're young, still trying to figure out who we are and what's important to us. But for some, this is an ongoing problem that leaves them feeling empty and lost.

Furthermore, if you have a mental health problem, you may experience low self-esteem or shame that can further contribute to this lack of identity, as well as dysregulated emotions. By increasing your awareness and acceptance of your internal experience through mindfulness, you can come to know yourself better, as you observe (nonjudgmentally) your thoughts, emotions, and physical sensations. This will help you feel better regulated—and like a more secure, integrated person.

What Are Your Reasons for Practicing Mindfulness?

You've learned a lot in the last few pages, so take a moment now to consider your reasons for practicing mindfulness. The clearer you are about why you're doing something, the more likely you'll be to do it, so make some notes here about how mindfulness will be helpful for you.

_____

_____

_____

Hopefully you've learned something about mindfulness that will motivate you to not just read through these pages, but to put what you're learning into practice! Now, let's turn to building this skill so you can continue learning how to manage your emotions.

How to Practice Mindfulness

While the idea of mindfulness may seem simple—doing one thing at a time, in the present moment, with your full attention, and with acceptance—putting it into practice is challenging for most people. Most of us have not learned this type of focus, and it's often in opposition to how our brains have been trained: most of us grew up in a society in which multitasking is something to brag about! Of course, technology nowadays makes mindfulness even more challenging, as we constantly divide our attention between a conversation we're having and the text or email we're sending while we're reading our newsfeed, listening to a podcast, and so on. Mindfulness is likely going to be a new way of living your life.

Throughout this book you'll have lots of opportunity to practice mindfulness, as this skill is helpful in many different ways and will come up often as you learn about ways to manage your emotions. Here's your first opportunity to practice mindfulness. Since this workbook's focus is regulating emotions, it makes sense to begin with a mindfulness practice that will help you start to learn more about your emotions and how you experience them in your body, which is one of the first steps in identifying emotions accurately.

Practice: Mindfulness of Emotions

To prepare for this practice, you might want to read the following script to yourself a couple of times so it comes more naturally for you when you start to practice. You might choose to record yourself reading the script so you can play it back to guide you through the practice until you get the hang of it, or you might have someone read it out loud to you.

> Start by sitting in a comfortable position, taking a dignified posture: your back fairly straight against the chair, your feet flat on the floor. (If you have physical pain issues, just do your best to adopt a posture that you'll be able to stay in.) Take a couple of deep breaths. Our breathing can become shallow when we're having a strong emotion, so try to feel your belly expand as you inhale. When you're ready, let your attention slowly move through your body from your head to fingertips and toes, scanning your body for places you're holding tension. It's common to clench your jaw or to literally sit on the edge of your seat if you're feeling a difficult emotion, so just observe whatever is happening in your body.

Allow yourself to become aware of any emotion that's with you right now. (If you don't notice anything, continue to scan through your body until you do notice something, however small or neutral it might seem.) Where do you feel it most strongly? There might be one or several places in your body where you feel the emotion. Just be curious about the sensations, exploring them with a sense of openness as best as you can. It's natural to notice yourself wanting to avoid or resist the feelings and sensations, especially if they're uncomfortable, but see if you can be with them with acceptance and curiosity instead, just for a moment. Remember to breathe.

Now see if you can put nonjudgmental words to your experience: describe what you notice in your body. For example, you might describe the quality of the feeling as "tight," "butterflies," "knot," or "hard"; describe the size of the feeling (small, medium, large); or notice a temperature to the emotion that you can label as "hot" or "cold" or somewhere in between. Go with whatever feels right; you're just listening to your body in this moment, observing the sensations that are present and the emotions they might reveal. You're not trying to make anything happen, nor are you trying to stop anything from happening.

You may be able to put a label on the emotion, like "grief," "shame," "bored," or "anxious." Label it if you can; if you can't put a name on it, just notice that. If you notice a thought or a story come up that's related to this emotion (for example, remembering something hurtful you did or said that has triggered feelings of shame for you), just notice that without judging as best as you can, and bring your attention back to whatever physical sensations are most prominent in your body right now.

If an emotion feels uncomfortable or distressing, see if you can just breathe into it, and continue to observe it, reminding yourself that it isn't permanent: emotions come and go. If it gets to be too much, you can leave the practice and come back to it another time. Ultimately, you can do this practice for as short or long a time as you'd like, letting your thoughts and emotions go and staying connected with your body.

This practice will help you recognize the different components of your emotions, so that over time you'll be able to accurately label them (we'll come back to the importance of that in later chapters). For now, let's get you thinking about the practice you just did by answering the following questions.

As you did this exercise, what did you notice in your body?

_____

_____

_____

What did you notice about your thoughts?

_____

_____

_____

What did you notice about your emotions?

_____

_____

_____

Were you able to distinguish between the physical, mental, and emotional parts of your experience?

_____

_____

Did you notice the emotions change in any way?

_____

_____

Did you notice any thoughts that brought up or intensified an emotion or physical sensation?

_____

_____

Hopefully this exercise has given you a felt sense of what it's like to pay attention to what's happening now, within yourself, with an attitude of openness and acceptance. It's important to remember that paying full attention to what you're doing in the present moment is only one part of mindfulness. The other part of this skill is *accepting* whatever you happen to notice in the present moment. It's usually quite challenging for us to experience something without judging it. For instance, when we look outside at the weather, most of us probably apply labels like "nice" or "awful" rather than simply observing it, as in *The sun is shining* or *It's raining*. Maybe you found yourself judging when you were observing body sensations, trying to avoid or ignore them or labeling them as "bad" or as something you "shouldn't" feel. If so, keep working to approach what you observe without judgment—it's all part of being mindful!

This practice is just one of an infinite number of ways to practice mindfulness. Let's look at some other ways to practice.

Formal and Informal Mindfulness Practices

There are two types of mindfulness practice. *Formal* practices, like the mindfulness of emotions practice you just did, require us to set aside a certain amount of time so that we can do a specific practice. They usually have us turning inward in some way: noticing our body, breath, emotions, physical sensations, and so on. Any guided mindfulness practice, like a body scan or a guided imagery exercise, is a formal practice. Later in this chapter you'll have an opportunity to do another formal practice, the counting breaths practice.

Informal mindfulness practices, on the other hand, involve bringing mindfulness to tasks or activities we're doing (for example, brushing your teeth, having a conversation, or driving). Informal practices help us to live our lives more mindfully—in the present moment, with our full attention, and with acceptance. Some practices, such as walking or eating, can either be formal or informal, depending on how you choose to practice them.

It's important to make time for both types of practice; while it's helpful to live your life more mindfully, being more present and accepting, the formal exercises (even short ones) will often give you a deeper understanding of your internal experiences. Here are the steps to follow when doing any kind of mindfulness practice, whether formal or informal.

Step 1: Choose what you'll focus on. This can be literally anything, as the ways of practicing mindfulness are limitless. If you're new to mindfulness, it can be helpful to start with something more concrete, like listening to music, going for a walk, petting your dog, or doing a guided mindfulness practice (There are lots of apps for this!).

Step 2: Start focusing on the activity you've chosen. If you're listening to music, start listening to the song; if you're walking, notice the feel of your body as you walk; or pay attention to what's around you, noticing the color of the sky, hearing the sound of birds, and so on.

Step 3: Notice *when* your attention wanders. This is to be expected and is fairly inevitable; it's what our brains do. What's important is that, at some point, you realize this has happened. It may take only a second, or you may find a few minutes have passed before you notice; regardless of how long it takes, just notice that your mind has wandered.

Step 4: As best as you can without judging, bring your attention back to the activity. Don't judge yourself for wandering, or for whatever distracted you, just bring your attention back to your focus. This can be difficult, because many of us have a tendency to be hard on ourselves, and we may judge ourselves for not doing it "right." But rather than falling back into this old pattern, see if you can accept this experience as an opportunity to come back to the present. (If you're already judging, do your best to just notice that, and let it go, bringing your attention back to the activity.)

And then repeat steps 3 and 4 over and over again! You may notice that your attention has wandered several times in just one minute, and that's natural. What's important is that you continue to notice these events, and you nonjudgmentally bring your attention back to the present moment as best as you can.

What Will Your Practice Look Like?

It's important to consider how you'll start practicing mindfulness. To make mindfulness as approachable as possible, I recommend that people who are new to mindfulness start with informal practice. If that makes sense for you, take some time to consider what activities you currently do that you're able to really engage in. If you can start practicing mindfulness with something you're naturally able to throw yourself into, the practice will be a little bit less difficult, which can be a nice way to start. The following list includes examples of moments when mindfulness tends to come more naturally for some of my clients. Check off any of the activities that you're able to really engage in, that tend to hold your attention without you having to make a real effort to stay in the present moment:

☐ Playing with a pet

☐ Hiking or walking

☐ Playing a musical instrument

☐ Playing a sport

☐ Watching an engrossing show

☐ Reading

☐ Dancing

☐ Having a discussion with someone about a topic you find very interesting

☐ Spending time with your favorite people

Other activities you find you're able to engage in, without your attention wandering much:

_____   _____

_____   _____

Next, choose one of these activities to do mindfully, following the four steps just described. Two-minute practices are a nice way to start, and over time you might also want to begin incorporating periods of formal practice into a daily routine.

Some people find that keeping track of their practice can help them make it part of a routine, and doing so can also draw your attention to things that arise during your practice that might provide important information about yourself. The following sample Mindfulness Log Sheet provides some ideas of the tracking you may want to do, and the blank one (which you can also download at this book's website: http://www.newharbinger.com/49647) is for you to use to track your practice.

Mindfulness Log Sheet

Date	How I Practiced	How Long I Practiced	What I Noticed About My Attention
2/14/21	Counting breaths practice	5 minutes	I wandered a lot, stressed out due to work; was eventually able to calm myself with this.
2/15/21	Progressive muscle relaxation	20 minutes	I fell asleep!
2/15/21	Brushing my teeth	1.5 minutes	I was distracted; not used to thinking about my teeth when I brush them.
2/17/21	Body scan	15 minutes	This was relaxing; also helped me notice emotions I didn't realize I was feeling.
2/18/21	Petting my dog	2 minutes	We both enjoyed it; she looks into my eyes as I pet her and I feel such love for her!
2/20/21	Talking to my mom on the phone	15 minutes	I noticed worry thoughts and sadness since I don't get to see my parents often and I know they won't be around forever. I tried to come back to the present and focus on what we were talking about, but it's hard.
2/20/21	Driving home from work	30 minutes off and on	I noticed a lot of judgments because I was in a hurry to get home and people were driving more slowly than I'd like. I took some deep breaths and worked on changing the judgments, and this helped with my frustration.

Mindfulness Log Sheet

Date	How I Practiced	How Long I Practiced	What I Noticed About My Attention

Rescue Skill: Counting Breaths

The rescue skill I'll leave you with here is a formal mindfulness practice called "counting breaths." In this practice we silently count our inhalations and exhalations, starting at one and ending at ten, and cycling back through those numbers: inhale, count the number one in your mind; exhale, count the number two; inhale, think the number three; and so on until you get to ten, then start back at one. As you do this practice, you'll notice that your mind wanders—and that's to be expected! Just notice you've wandered and bring yourself back to counting your breaths. If you find yourself multitasking—counting your breaths as you think about other things—just notice that, without judging, and do your best to refocus on counting your inhalations and exhalations (if you struggle with this, you might visualize the numbers as you count to help you focus).

To help quickly regulate yourself, add paced breathing, which you learned in chapter 1, to this practice. Remember that making your exhale longer than your inhale activates your parasympathetic nervous system (PNS), helping you feel calmer, so as you count your inhales and exhales from one to ten, see if you can also make your exhale a little bit longer than your inhale. This mindfulness exercise can also provide a bit of a distraction from distressing thoughts as you count.

Set a timer for two minutes and try this practice, then answer the following questions.

What did you notice about your experience as you counted your breaths?

_____

_____

Were you able to do the full two minutes? Did you notice urges to stop? If you did, were you able to keep going?

_____

_____

Did your attention wander? If it did, did you notice where it went? Make some notes about what you noticed.

_____

_____

Remember, mindfulness is difficult for most people at first, so be patient with yourself. If two minutes is too long, start with one minute instead. If you found yourself feeling too emotional to count your breaths, you can also do a forward bend or use one of the other reregulating skills before you start the practice. And know that mindfulness will come more naturally over time!

Wrapping Up

In this chapter I introduced you to the foundational skill of mindfulness. Of course just reading about this skill isn't likely to get you very far; the bulk of the work will be bringing it into your life as best as you can so that over time it will start to come more naturally.

In the next chapter, we'll build on what we started working on here by delving more deeply into the topic of emotions: how to accurately identify and name them; differentiating between thoughts, emotions, and behaviors; and learning about what emotions do for you. This foundation will prepare you for the work to come with reregulating yourself during an emotional hijacking, and with preventing hijacks from happening in the first place. So practice, practice, practice, and when you're ready to move on, turn the page.

CHAPTER 4

Getting to Know Your Emotions

In the last chapter we looked at the skill of mindfulness, and you've been working on increasing your self-awareness through mindfulness practice. This is an important step to prepare you for the work we'll be doing in this chapter: learning more about emotions.

Do you find yourself walking around in an emotional fog, not aware of the feelings you're having until it's too late and they're already taking over—you lose it on your partner, the kids, or the dog, or you burst into tears at the slight critical tone in your boss's voice? In order to tame emotions, we must be able to name them (Siegel 2014); this is why you need to get to know your emotions better. To help with this, we'll be taking a closer look at some of the basic human emotions, their purpose, and information and strategies to help you accurately identify and label them, including exercises to help you unravel their different components.

There's a lot of information in this chapter, and you might be a little overwhelmed by it, but think of this chapter as the place where you need to start. I'm helping you to arm yourself with knowledge, and with knowledge comes power, which will help you reduce that emotional dysregulation (aka the emotional hijack or meltdown). Let's start with the basics: what an emotion actually is.

What Is an Emotion?

Although we often refer to emotions as "feelings," the feeling aspect is just one part of the experience. Emotions are, in fact, *full system responses* that involve thoughts, physical sensations, urges, and behaviors (Linehan 1993). Because there's so much going on when we're feeling an emotion, it can be difficult to tell the difference between how we *feel*, what we *think* (the thoughts), and what we *do* (the behaviors). For example, if you're experiencing the emotion of anger, you're going to *feel* angry, which would include physical sensations in your body (like tense muscles, racing heart, or shakiness). Your *thought* might be *It's not fair that I have to do all of this extra work just to handle my emotions!* And the *behavior* might be to throw this book at the wall. *Urges,* by the way, are a combination of emotions and thoughts. In the previous example, for instance, the urge would be a combination of the *emotion* of anger and the *thought* of throwing the book, both of which precede the action.

The Function of Emotions

It's important to know that all emotions serve a purpose; they've helped us to survive as a species, and, as painful as they can be at times, we need them. Having an understanding of the function of emotions can help you be more accepting of them. Here are the three jobs that our emotions do for us (Linehan 2014).

Emotions motivate and organize us for action. The urges associated with many emotions are hardwired (for example, that biological fight-or-flight response of the sympathetic nervous system, or SNS, is a response that's hardwired in the human brain). What this means is that emotions save us time when we need to act quickly in certain situations; this is especially helpful when we don't have time to stop and think things through logically.

Can you think of a time when you found yourself suddenly caught up in a fear response? I recall an early morning walk with my two small dogs, when we suddenly encountered two larger dogs I had never seen before. There were no people around, and my flight response kicked in: I quickly scooped up my little ones and began a fast walk away from the unknown dogs. I didn't stop to think about what I was doing or to assess the threat; my brain just propelled me to act.

Sometimes strong emotions help us overcome obstacles: if the two larger dogs had attacked, for example, my fight response may have caused me to fight those two dogs in order to protect my beloved pets. Emotions often motivate us in this way (for example, you feel angry about something happening in your workplace, and that anger motivates you to report unsafe working conditions, make a complaint to HR regarding harassing behavior by a colleague, or have a conversation with your boss about a raise or some time off).

Emotions help us communicate to others. Our nonverbal communication (body language, facial expression, and tone of voice) makes up a large part of what we communicate to others. The nonverbal cues that go along with our emotions are also hardwired into us and can actually communicate things to others faster than our words. This can be helpful at times; for example, you don't have to tell someone you're feeling sad because they recognize this by the tears in your eyes, the tone of your voice, your slumped posture, and so on. But nonverbal communication can also be problematic: if you don't want to communicate your emotion to others, it can sometimes be difficult to avoid doing so.

Some people encounter problems if they've gotten too good at putting a mask on to hide the emotion they're experiencing. Is this you? Are you a good actor, telling your partner or friend that you're not annoyed with them, while inside you're actually seething? While we all need to put a mask on at times—we can't always wear our hearts on our sleeves—some people become so adept at masking their true feelings that they don't realize they're doing it. One problem with this is that they might end up feeling invalidated when the people around them aren't responding to how they're really feeling, not realizing it's because others can't tell!

Emotions provide us with information. Sometimes our emotions give us helpful information about a situation. Think about times you've had a gut feeling or a vibe about something. A first impression of someone you've just met is a great example. Have you ever caught yourself thinking *I'm not sure what it is about that person, but I have a good feeling about them,* or *I can't put my finger on it, they just give me the creeps?*

It's important, of course, to remember that this vibe is just a feeling, not a fact, and to therefore treat the feeling as just one piece of a puzzle. How often have you been wrong with a first impression? For instance, maybe you came to dislike a person you originally had a good feeling about. Likewise, just because you sometimes *feel* unloved by your partner doesn't mean they don't love you; just because you *feel* anxious that you won't be able to make changes in your life doesn't mean you can't do it. Think of your emotion as another sense to consider in the bigger picture. Consider this analogy: If you're cooking a stew on the stove, you're smelling it and you're looking at it, and at some point you're also going to taste it. You rely on as many senses as you can to provide you with information about how the stew is turning out. Like one of our five senses, our emotions can provide us with important information in life's situations, helping us evaluate how best to respond.

Now that you have an understanding of what emotions do for us, let's start helping you to identify and name them more accurately.

Naming Emotions

Researchers still disagree about which emotions are "basic" human emotions—those that are universal experiences and are hardwired into us. In DBT, ten basic emotions have been identified: anger, fear, sadness, guilt, shame, envy, jealousy, disgust, love, and happiness (Linehan 2014). I won't be offering an in-depth analysis of all of these emotions, just the ones that most commonly contribute to emotion dysregulation. So, keep in mind that if you finish this chapter and still have questions about some of the emotions that cause you difficulties, you may need to do more work in this area outside of what's offered here. For some people, happiness, love, and other pleasurable emotions are problematic (for instance, some people might engage in impulsive behaviors when they're feeling happiness or love, whereas others might have beliefs like they're not deserving of these emotions). Please keep in mind that you can use the skills in this book to help you manage even the more pleasurable emotions.

Let's start with a fun exercise to get you practicing naming emotions. In bold, you'll see the DBT list of basic emotions followed by a list of other emotion names. In the blank space, write the basic emotion you think the emotion is a synonym for. I provided an example to get you started. As an interesting experiment, guess what you think your score will be: _____/20 (_____%).

Anger   Fear   Sadness   Guilt   Shame   Envy   Jealousy   Disgust   Happiness   Love

Example: Trepidation	Fear
1. Enraged	
2. Nervous	
3. Joyful	
4. Irritated	
5. Frustrated	
6. Remorseful	
7. Miserable	
8. Grossed out	
9. Regretful	
10. Repulsed	
11. Covetous	
12. Terrified	
13. Triumphant	
14. Possessive	
15. Adoration	
16. Self-conscious	
17. Humiliated	
18. Annoyed	
19. Anxious	
20. Self-loathing	

Answers

1.	Anger	11.	Envy
2.	Fear	12.	Fear
3.	Happiness	13.	Happiness
4.	Anger	14.	Jealousy
5.	Anger	15.	Love
6.	Guilt	16.	Shame
7.	Sadness	17.	Shame
8.	Disgust	18.	Anger
9.	Guilt	19.	Fear
10.	Disgust	20.	Shame

Score: _____/20 (_____%)

How did you do in relation to how you thought you'd do? By the way, just because you struggle to manage your emotions at times doesn't necessarily mean that you don't name your emotions accurately. And if you did well with this exercise, it doesn't necessarily mean that you accurately label your emotions when you're actually experiencing them. Intense emotions often have the effect of limiting our ability to think straight! But this exercise might give you at least an idea as to whether identifying emotions might be a problem for you.

Let's move on to some information you need to know about emotions to learn how to regulate them.

What You Need to Know About Emotions

From a DBT perspective, every emotion serves a purpose or can be *justified* at times, meaning that they make sense given the situation. In the following Emotion Reference Sheets, you'll learn about the function of some of the more common painful emotions; the urges, thoughts, and body sensations associated with each; and different words for each. You'll also have an opportunity to consider your own experience of these emotions, since everyone experiences emotions differently.

I don't expect you to remember all of the following information (Linehan 2014)! Because of that, when you experience an emotion you'll want to refer back to these reference sheets so you gradually learn how to name your emotions accurately (or confirm that you're already labeling them accurately). I suggest that you thoroughly read these reference sheets now, and come back to them periodically to help you complete the worksheets provided later in this chapter.

Anger

Anger's purpose. Anger arises when someone or something is getting in the way of you moving toward a goal, or when you or someone you care about is being attacked, threatened, insulted, or hurt by others.

What anger does. Anger typically causes people to become aggressive, possibly causing them to physically or verbally attack what they see as dangerous, to make the threat go away. When the human race was evolving and there were constant threats in the environment, anger helped us survive.

Example of when anger is justified. You get passed over for a promotion even though you have seniority and your performance appraisals have been good. Your boss has prevented you from reaching a goal, so it makes sense and is justified that you feel angry in this situation.

Examples of anger thoughts. *This is ridiculous. They can't get away with this; that promotion should have been mine. They don't know what they're doing.* Usually anger thoughts involve judgments (like *This is ridiculous*), thinking what's happening shouldn't be happening or that people shouldn't be the way they are.

Activity: Describe Your Anger

Think of a recent time when you felt angry, and describe the situation.

_____

_____

Body sensations. Take a look at these physical sensations connected to anger and check off any that you experienced in this situation.

- ☐ Tense or tight muscles, such as clenching fists or jaw (your body preparing you to fight in a dangerous situation)

- ☐ Trembling or shaking

- ☐ Racing heart

- ☐ Increased breathing rate

- ☐ Change in body temperature, which might lead to feeling hot or cold

- ☐ Other: _____

What urges did you notice when you were in the situation you described?

_____

What did you actually do? _____

Other words for anger. Circle any of the words that describe how you felt in this situation.

Annoyed	Bitter	Bothered	Outraged
Frustrated	Mad	Incensed	Hostile
Irritated	Irate	Cross	Peeved
Exasperated	Furious	Impatient	Indignant
Resentful	Aggravated	Enraged	

If you can think of other words that fit better, add them here: _____

It's important to note that just because a feeling is justified doesn't mean you should act on the urges associated with it. For example, you can feel anger at your boss for not giving you what you want and choose not to respond to your urge to quit your job or verbally abuse your boss (this skill will be covered in chapter 7).

Fear and Anxiety

Fear is different from but very related to anxiety. Fear and anxiety essentially feel the same physically; the main difference between them is that fear is present focused and related to a specific threat, motivating you to act by triggering the fight-or-flight response, which helps you survive in dangerous situations. Anxiety, however, comes up when there's a more general threat you're worrying about, something that hasn't happened yet and may never happen. It also comes up when there's something you might reasonably expect to happen and you expect the results to be catastrophic, or out of proportion with reality. So, if you're driving on the highway and you're thinking *What if someone hits me?* you're likely going to feel anxious.

While there are definitely times when fear is justified, there isn't really a time when you *should* feel anxious, or when you can say that your anxiety would be justified, because anxiety involves a fear of something that isn't a real threat—even if it feels that way! But it's important to know that some anxiety is helpful, because without it you wouldn't be cautious while you're driving, making you less likely to react quickly by braking when a car cuts you off. Without some anxiety, you might take more risks, like driving dangerously. So we're not trying to get rid of anxiety (or any emotion, for that matter, since all emotions serve a purpose), but if you have anxiety regularly—or to the extreme, such as by having panic attacks—you want you to be able to manage it better, instead of letting it control you.

Fear's purpose. Fear comes up when there's a danger to your health, your safety, or your well-being or to that of someone you care about.

What fear does. Fear motivates you to act to protect yourself or those you care about.

Example of when fear is justified. You're driving down a busy freeway at seventy miles per hour and you see traffic coming to a dead stop not far in front of you. Fear is justified because your safety is threatened.

Examples of anxious thoughts. Anxious thoughts are future-focused catastrophizing or worry thoughts often consisting of *what-ifs: What if I make a fool of myself? What if I can't do it? What if that car hits me?*

Activity: Describe Your Anxiety

Think of a recent time when you felt fearful or anxious, and describe the situation.

_____

_____

Body sensations. Take a look at the following physical sensations that can be connected to fear and anxiety and check off those you experienced in the situation.

☐ Tense or tight muscles (your body preparing you to flee a dangerous situation)

☐ Trembling or shaking muscles

☐ Racing heart

☐ Increased breathing rate

☐ Change in body temperature, which might lead to feeling hot or cold

☐ Other: _____

Urges and behaviors. With fear, urges and behaviors usually involve running away from the threat to protect yourself or the people you care about. With anxiety, urges and behaviors usually involve avoiding a situation (like choosing not to go to work because you're worried that you'll have a panic attack and make a fool of yourself) or escaping the situation if you're already in it (like leaving work early, because you're feeling anxious).

What urges did you notice when you were in the situation you described?

_____

What did you actually do? _____

Other words for fear. Circle any of the words that describe how you felt in this situation.

Trepidation	Apprehensive	Disturbed	Edgy	Anxious
Panicky	Nervous	Stressed	Jumpy	Concerned
Terrified	Worried	Startled	Jittery	Uneasy
Scared	Dread	Alarmed	Troubled	

If you can think of other words that fit better, add them here: _____

As you recalled your experience of fear or anxiety, did you notice a similarity to what you experience when you feel angry? The body sensations can be very much the same, which is one reason why it can be easy to mix up feelings of fear or anxiety and anger!

Sadness

Sadness's purpose. Sadness is the emotion felt when things aren't the way you expected them to be or when you've experienced a loss of some sort.

What sadness does. This is the emotion that encourages people around you to try to be of help or to offer support. It might also motivate you to try to regain what you've lost, or to seek comfort from others.

Examples of when sadness is justified. You didn't get a job you really wanted, your partner is ending your relationship, or someone close to you receives a diagnosis of a terminal illness. Sadness is justified in these situations because you've experienced loss, and because things aren't as you had expected them to be.

Examples of sadness thoughts. When we're feeling sad our tendency is to focus on the loss we've experienced and on the disappointment we feel. Some examples of sad thoughts include *Things are hopeless, I'm not worthwhile, I'm unloved,* or *I have no one.*

Activity: Describe Your Sadness

Think of a recent time when you felt sad, and describe the situation:

_____

_____

Body sensations. Take a look at these physical sensations connected to sadness and check off the ones you experienced in this situation.

- ☐ Tightness in chest or throat
- ☐ Heaviness in chest or heart
- ☐ Tears in eyes
- ☐ Slumped posture
- ☐ Tired or heavy body
- ☐ Other: _____

Urges and behaviors. Urges and behaviors associated with feeling sad often involve withdrawing from others, isolating ourselves, or crying.

What urges did you notice when you were in the situation you described?

_____

What did you actually do? _____

Other words for sadness. Circle any of the words that describe how you felt in this situation.

Disappointed	Miserable	Down	Downhearted
Discouraged	Despair	Distressed	Unhappy
Distraught	Grief	Depressed	Despondent
Resigned	Sorrow	Heartbroken	
Hopeless	Anguish	Glum	

If you can think of other words that fit, add them here: _____

Guilt

We often feel guilt and shame in the same situations, and many aspects of these emotions are similar, which can cause us to confuse them. These two emotions are very common for people who experience emotion dysregulation, and shame especially can be very powerful in keeping people dysregulated. We'll cover shame in the next reference sheet.

Guilt's purpose. Guilt is the feeling that comes up when you've done something that goes against your values and you judge your behavior.

What guilt does. Guilt motivates you to make amends and prevents you from acting a certain way in the future.

Examples of when guilt is justified. You say something to purposely hurt your partner during an argument, or your boss overpays you and you decide to keep the money and not tell them. Your behavior in both situations doesn't match your values, so you feel guilty.

Examples of guilt thoughts. When feeling guilty we tend to think judgmental thoughts about our behavior: *That was wrong, I shouldn't have done that. If only I had done things differently. It's my fault.* We might also dwell on past behaviors when feeling guilty.

Activity: Describe Your Guilt

Think of a recent time when you felt guilt, and describe the situation.

_____

_____

Body sensations. Take a look at the following body sensations connected to guilt and check off any that you experienced in this situation.

- ☐ Feeling jittery or agitated

- ☐ Hot, flushed face

- ☐ Bowed head

- ☐ Other: _____

Urges and behaviors. When feeling guilty, you often want to make amends (apologizing to your partner, for example) to try to make up for what you did.

What urges did you notice when you were in the situation you described?

_____

What did you actually do? _____

Other words for guilt. Circle any of the words that describe how you felt in this situation.

Remorseful	Regretful	Contrition
Apologetic	Self-reproach	Sorry

If you can think of other words that fit better, add them here: _____

Shame

Shame's purpose. Shame protects you by keeping you connected to others. Shame develops when you judge yourself for something you've done, or for something about yourself as a person that you fear might cause people to reject you if they knew about it.

What shame does. Shame causes you to hide—your behavior, or that characteristic of yourself—so you can remain connected to people who are important to you. Shame is also the emotion that comes up to stop you from doing that same behavior again in future. If people know about your behavior (or characteristic), shame causes you to try to make amends in those relationships.

Examples of when shame is justified. You engage in a target behavior (like drinking, using drugs, or gambling) as a means of dealing with your emotions, and you hide your behavior so others won't reject you for it. Whether or not shame is justified in this example depends on who you're hiding from. Some people might reject you for what you did, in which case shame is justified; it's causing you to hide the behavior, protecting you by keeping you connected. But others (like your significant other, your best friend, or your therapist) hopefully would not reject you, in which case shame would not be justified. Shame is also justified if you cheat on your partner, because quite possibly they will reject you if they find out, and shame is there to stop you from doing the same behavior again in future.

You may also experience shame if there's something that makes you different from others, or at least you believe it makes you different. This could be your sexual or gender identity, a mental health or addiction problem, your religion, or a particular belief or opinion you hold. Hiding that part of yourself protects you from being rejected by others. It's sometimes difficult to tell if shame is justified or not, because this emotion involves an element of knowing the opinions and values of others, and what they might think if they knew about this thing. For instance, many still attach stigma to mental illness, and if your best friend has previously told you about their coworker who "uses their depression as an excuse all the time," or they insist that there's "no such thing as mental illness," then you're likely to keep quiet about your emotional problems in order to avoid their judgment. On the other hand, if your boss has confided in you about their own anxious thoughts, or the fact that their child has been hospitalized for mental health problems, you'll be more certain that you can talk to them without fear of rejection.

More often than not, shame is not actually justified. It often comes up, though, because shame is the awful, soul-sucking feeling that we feel when we judge ourselves. So instead of thinking *I shouldn't have said that to my partner* (causing guilt), you're thinking *What kind of person am I that I said that to my partner?* or *I'm awful.* Judging yourself for something you've done or for something you feel is defective about you will cause you to feel shame.

I mentioned earlier that we often tend to confuse guilt and shame. One reason for this is that we often feel both at the same time, when we judge our behavior (leading to feelings of guilt) and we judge ourselves for having done that behavior (causing us to feel shame).

Examples of shame thoughts. When we feel ashamed we're usually judging ourselves in some way: *I'm defective. There's something wrong with me. If others knew the real me they would leave. I'm an awful person. I'm a failure.* With shame there is also often an element of fearing that others will reject us.

Activity: Describe Your Shame

Think of a recent time when you felt shame, and describe the situation.

_____

_____

Body sensations. Take a look at these physical sensations connected to shame and check off any that you experienced in this situation.

☐   Pain in the pit of the stomach

☐   Slumped posture, bowed head

☐   Hot, flushed face

☐   Sense of dread

☐   Other: _____

Urges and behaviors. Shame can make you want to crawl under the nearest rock, hiding and isolating your-self from others. Taken to the extreme, it can cause thoughts of suicide. It can also be difficult to make eye contact with others when you're feeling shame.

What urges did you notice when you were in the situation you described?

_____

What did you actually do? _____

Other words for shame. Circle any of the words that describe how you felt in this situation.

Mortified

Self-loathing

Self-disgust

If you can think of other words that fit better, add them here: _____

There aren't really many other words for shame, although sometimes we use "embarrassed" or "humiliated" to describe the emotion, even though both are very different from shame. Think of "embarrassed" as the feeling we have when we trip up the stairs or walk out of the bathroom with TP stuck to our foot: when we're embarrassed, we can laugh at ourselves or the situation later. "Humiliation" is a little closer to shame, but it also involves anger—the sense of someone having caused us to feel shame when we didn't deserve it. In this sense humiliation can be seen as more tolerable than shame because the anger drives us to talk to others about the situation and seek validation for our feelings, whereas shame keeps us disconnected and hiding.

Envy

Envy and jealousy are two more emotions that are often confused with each other, but they are very distinct.

Envy's purpose. Envy is the emotion that usually comes up when an individual or group of people has something that you want.

What envy does. Healthy envy motivates us to work hard to get what we want. For example, if I envy a coworker who received recognition at work, it drives me to work harder so that I might also be recognized in some way. But envy can also play out in unhealthy urges, such as acting in ways to try to make the other person look bad to others, judging the person, trying to take away or ruin what the other person has, and so on.

Example of when envy is justified. You have feelings for your best friend's partner—that is, you envy your best friend for that relationship. If you were never part of the in-crowd at school, you may have been envious of the popular people (and this may still be happening!). Seeing someone who seems to have everything—lots of money, a great career, a beautiful house, a happy marriage—and wanting (understandably!) what that person has is justified.

Examples of envy thoughts. *It's not fair; why can't I have that? Why do they get all the luck and I get nothing but suffering in life?* When envy is accompanied by feelings of happiness for the other person, it can be quite healthy. As noted earlier, envy can motivate us to work hard to get the things we want: *I'm happy that my coworker got that promotion, but damn I wish that had been me!* When envy isn't accompanied by those feelings, but rather by feelings of anger, it can be detrimental and cause us to get stuck in feelings of self-pity and unhealthy behaviors.

Activity: Describe Your Envy

Think of a recent time when you felt envy, and describe the situation.

_____

_____

Body sensations. Take a look at these physical sensations connected to envy and check off any that you experienced in this situation.

- ☐ Tight or rigid muscles

- ☐ Teeth clenching

- ☐ Mouth tightening

- ☐ Face flushing

- ☐ Pain in the pit of the stomach

- ☐ Other: _____

Urges and behaviors. Healthy urges and behaviors related to envy usually involve pushing yourself to do more and try harder to improve yourself and your situation. Unhealthy urges and behaviors related to envy include attacking or criticizing the person you envy; doing something to try to make that person fail, look bad to others, or lose what they have; or avoiding seeing or interacting with the person.

What urges did you notice when you were in the situation you described?

_____

What did you actually do? _____

Other words for envy. Circle any of the words that describe how you felt in this situation.

Craving	Hunger	Desirous	Resentful
Covetous	Wanting	Longing	

If you can think of words that fit better, add them here: _____

Jealousy

Jealousy's purpose. Like all of the emotions we're looking at, jealousy is a basic emotion that has been identified in infants and can therefore be described as hardwired in the human brain. This emotion arises when an important relationship or sense of belonging is in danger of being lost or taken away.

What jealousy does. Jealousy typically causes people to try to control others in order to protect what's "theirs" (whether accurate or not!), and to not share the people or things they fear they'll lose.

Examples of when jealousy is justified. You find out that your partner has been talking to their ex. Or, you reached out to your three closest friends to see if they'd like to get together, but no one responded; then weeks later your best friend lets slip that they and those two other friends met last week without you—ouch.

Examples of jealousy thoughts. *They're going to leave me. No one cares about me. I'm going to lose everything.* Jealousy can also be thought of as anxiety about losing someone or something that's important to you.

Activity: Describe Your Jealousy

Think of a recent time when you felt jealous, and describe the situation.

_____

_____

Body sensations. Take a look at these physical sensations connected to jealousy and check off any that you experienced in this situation.

- ☐ Racing heart

- ☐ Breathlessness

- ☐ Choking sensation

- ☐ Lump in throat

- ☐ Tense or tight muscles, such as clenching teeth

- ☐ Other: _____

Urges and behaviors. Urges and behaviors associated with feeling jealous might involve being violent or threatening violence toward the person you feel threatened by; trying to control the person you're afraid of losing, including interrogating and spying on them and snooping through their belongings; accusing the person you're afraid of losing of being unfaithful or disloyal; behaving in a clinging, dependent way; or increasing demonstrations of love, like trying to spend more time together.

What urges did you notice when you were in the situation you described?

_____

What did you actually do? _____

Other words for jealousy. Circle any of the words that describe how you felt in this situation.

Protective	Possessive	Distrustful	Clingy
Suspicious	Covetous	Rivalrous	Insecure

If you can think of other words that fit better, add them here: _____

Now that you have a better understanding of some of the painful emotions you might be experiencing, let's talk about what to do with this knowledge. Again, I know this might feel like a lot—and it is. We often don't really learn the ins and outs of emotions like this when we're growing up; instead we tend to label our emotions and just assume that we know what we feel rather than exploring them further. Emotions can get really complicated for a number of reasons, which we'll continue to look at as we move forward. But first, let's get you applying what you're learning by thinking about situations you encounter in your own life. The following Awareness of Emotions Worksheet will help you start to examine your emotions more closely, which will help you name the emotions accurately and understand them better. Fill out one of these worksheets when you have an emotion. Do this at least a couple of times each week in order to familiarize yourself with your experience of different emotions. It will be most helpful if you complete this worksheet as soon as possible after the emotionally charged situation. I included a sample worksheet for your reference, as well as a blank worksheet, which you can also download at this book's website: http://www.newharbinger.com/49647.

Awareness of Emotions Worksheet

Description of the situation that triggered the emotion (just the facts!):

My supervisor Tamara was off sick. Our secretary called me asking if I could help a client who had come in for an appointment with Tamara, not having received the message that she was away. I spoke to the client and was able to give them a document they had come to pick up; they left satisfied. On Tamara's return to the office the next day, she sent me an email reprimanding me for having intervened with her client and asking me not to do this again.

What thoughts did you have about this situation (including judgments, interpretations, assumptions)?

She's being a complete idiot! I did her a favor and provided good customer service; I didn't get anything out of it, but she's worried about me making her look bad. I know she hates me and she just wants me gone.

What physical sensations did you notice?

Heat in my body, heart racing, shallow breath, shaking, muscle tension.

What urges did you experience?

I wanted to yell at Tamara and tell her how selfish she is.

What did you actually do? I didn't say anything. I hid in my office because I don't want her to see how much this bothers me. I also don't want to rock the boat at work because I know she's doing her best to get rid of me.

What is the name of the emotion(s) you were experiencing? Anger and anxiety.

Awareness of Emotions Worksheet

Description of the situation that triggered the emotion (just the facts!):

_____

_____

_____

What thoughts did you have about this situation (including judgments, interpretations, assumptions)?

_____

_____

_____

What physical sensations did you notice?

_____

_____

What urges did you experience?

_____

_____

What did you actually do?

_____

_____

What is the name of the emotion(s) you were experiencing? _____

_____

As you complete this worksheet and get to know your experience of emotions better, it will be helpful for you to refer to the Emotion Reference Sheets provided in this chapter. For example, you may think you're feeling guilt but find, when you turn to the reference sheet on "guilt," that it doesn't quite match with your experience: you're not judging your *behavior*, but *yourself*, and it's actually shame you're feeling. Over time, completing the worksheet and reviewing the information about emotions will help improve your ability to identify what you're feeling.

There are other factors that can complicate our ability to name our emotions; for instance, we often feel more than one emotion in response to a situation. Also remember that emotions are full system responses, including not just the feeling but thoughts and behaviors as well—and it can be easy to confuse these different components. For example, often when I ask my clients how they feel, instead of telling me the emotion they're experiencing they offer a thought they're having: "I feel like this isn't fair!" or "I feel like my partner should be more understanding." These are thoughts attached to the emotions, but they're not emotions themselves.

Let's get you practicing the skill of differentiating between emotions, thoughts, and behaviors. In the following exercise, circle which word best describes each statement. Once again, why don't you predict your score: _____/20 (_____%). You can check your answers against the key that follows this exercise.

Practice: Knowing the Difference Between Emotions, Thoughts, Behaviors

1. Being afraid you'll lose a person you're close to.	Emotion	Thought	Behavior
2. Worrying about money.	Emotion	Thought	Behavior
3. Lashing out at someone.	Emotion	Thought	Behavior
4. Disappointment that you didn't get a job you applied for.	Emotion	Thought	Behavior
5. Believing it's not fair that you didn't get the job you applied for.	Emotion	Thought	Behavior
6. Yelling at someone.	Emotion	Thought	Behavior
7. Having guilt for yelling at that person.	Emotion	Thought	Behavior
8. Having a dream that you cheated on your partner.	Emotion	Thought	Behavior
9. Exchanging romantic messages with your ex.	Emotion	Thought	Behavior
10. Having the urge to drink alcohol.	Emotion	Thought	Behavior
11. Loving your dog.	Emotion	Thought	Behavior
12. Doing your chores.	Emotion	Thought	Behavior
13. Wanting to feel better.	Emotion	Thought	Behavior
14. Being frustrated that you're not feeling better.	Emotion	Thought	Behavior
15. Happiness.	Emotion	Thought	Behavior
16. Having an urge to scream.	Emotion	Thought	Behavior
17. Crying.	Emotion	Thought	Behavior
18. Punching the wall.	Emotion	Thought	Behavior
19. Being enraged.	Emotion	Thought	Behavior
20. Judging yourself as "stupid."	Emotion	Thought	Behavior

Answers

1. Emotion
2. Thought and emotion
3. Behavior
4. Emotion
5. Thought
6. Behavior
7. Emotion
8. Thought
9. Behavior
10. Thought and emotion

11. Emotion
12. Behavior
13. Thought
14. Emotion
15. Emotion
16. Thought and emotion
17. Behavior
18. Behavior
19. Emotion
20. Thought

Score: _____/20 (_____%)

How did you do in comparison to how you thought you'd do? Were you surprised? Remember that it's one thing to be able to differentiate between emotions, thoughts, and behaviors in a written exercise like this, and a completely different thing to be able to have this awareness in the heat of the moment. So don't get frustrated if you struggle with figuring things out during an emotional situation; it takes practice. Being able to untangle the various components of your emotions, though, is an important part of being able to manage them.

Rescue Skill: Acupressure Points

Before we wind things down with this chapter, let me give you a quick rescue skill to help you manage when emotions get intense. This is another skill that doesn't take a lot of thought or practice; you just have to remember to do it.

Many people are already familiar with using acupressure points to treat physical pain, but acupressure points can also help us feel a little calmer when emotions start to spike. The LI4 acupressure point, between your thumb and your index finger, activates endorphins in the body that help reduce stress. Using the index finger and thumb of your right hand, gently pinch the cushy part between the index finger and thumb of your left hand; use a deep, firm pressure to massage and stimulate the area for four to five seconds (you can also massage your right hand with your left).

Another acupressure point is located just under our collarbone. Massaging the little indent directly above the collarbone, between the breastbone and shoulder, can also help us to feel a little calmer. You can massage either side alone, or do both sides at once, adding in a bit of a self-hug, which can't do anything but help! And, incorporating paced breathing, which you already learned, with this self-massage will further activate a calming response in your body.

Wrapping Up

In this chapter you learned a lot of information about emotions. Much of this is setting the stage for skills to follow, so be sure to pay attention to your emotions, listening to their messages. Continue to use the Emotion Reference Sheets and the Awareness of Emotions Worksheet to learn more about your experience of emotions, and to learn how to name them accurately. You may think you know this stuff already, but I can't tell you how many times I've been working with someone who was convinced they were feeling one emotion and, as we explored it further together, realized they were actually feeling something else! Be sure to also keep working on differentiating between your emotions, thoughts, and behaviors. And now you have an additional rescue skill—acupressure points—you can use when you start to feel overwhelmed or out of control with your emotions.

Just a quick reminder here as you keep practicing the skills you've already learned in this workbook: when you're doing work like this, slower is better, because you'll be able to more fully absorb and put into practice what you're learning.

CHAPTER 5

Finding Your Internal Wisdom

In the last chapter you learned a lot about emotions, and we did some exercises to practice naming emotions and differentiating between emotions, thoughts, and behaviors. In this chapter we'll be looking at some skills to further increase your understanding of your emotions, and of yourself, in order to find your internal wisdom. We'll start by discussing the importance of taking a more balanced (dialectical) perspective to help keep emotions more manageable. We'll also look at the different thinking styles we all have, and you'll learn some ways to reduce your vulnerability to emotions.

Taking a More Balanced Perspective

You may have wondered what "dialectical" in *dialectical* behavior therapy means. *Dialectics* is about moving away from black-and-white thinking and finding the grays. Does the notion of black-and-white thinking resonate for you? Do you see yourself as an all-or-nothing thinker? (Hint: If you find yourself answering that question with "always" or "never," you might be a black-and-white thinker!)

Dialectics moves us toward a more balanced way of thinking, toward a more balanced way of living our life, and toward a more balanced way of feeling our emotions. You'll see this theme of balance throughout this book. Here's a great example of striving for balance in life: We might not like how things are, but we want to work on accepting our experience as it is, as well as on changing it when we can. Living with dialectics in mind is not about doing one or the other, but both.

When you find yourself getting caught up in extremes (like *This isn't fair!* or *My boss always treats me this way!*), you're not thinking dialectically. Most of us probably engage in all-or-nothing thinking at times. This is problematic because it can activate our emotions, getting us stuck in a one-sided perspective, unable to see other viewpoints, which often triggers anger, self-righteousness, and other painful emotions. (By the way, you may have noticed that throughout this workbook I refer to emotions as either "painful" or "pleasurable," rather than "negative" or "positive," in keeping with dialectics!)

Here are some tips to help you take a more balanced perspective:

- Remember that there are no absolute truths, only different perspectives, and that there's more than one side to every story. Practice looking for other points of view, seeing things from the perspectives of others.

- Don't assume you know what's going on in someone else's head. Instead, notice your assumptions and check them out. Similarly, don't expect others to read your mind.

- Accept that different opinions can be valid, and know that taking a balanced perspective doesn't necessarily mean you agree with the opinions of others!

- Move away from "either-or" thinking to "both-and" thinking, avoiding extremes (like "always" or "never"). Replacing the word "but" with "and" can be helpful with this. For example, in the sentence "I see your point, *but* this is how I feel…," the word "but" presses the delete button, so to speak, invalidating the other person's perspective. In the sentence "I see your point, *and* this is how I feel…," the word "and" allows for both perspectives to be possible at the same time.

Let's do an exercise to help you understand the concept of taking a balanced perspective. Read through the following scenarios and write out a nondialectical and a dialectical response for each. I've written some possible responses at the end of the section for you to compare yours to, but in keeping with dialectics, let's be clear that my responses aren't "right" and yours aren't "wrong"— they're just different! Here's an example to get you started.

Example scenario. Your partner gave you this workbook as a gift. What are your thoughts?

Nondialectical response: Why on earth would my partner give me this book? They must think I'm nuts. Clearly they can't handle my emotions!

Dialectical response: Hmm. My partner gave me this book about managing emotions. I know they've seen me struggle with emotions at times. Are they just trying to help, or is there an underlying message?

Scenario 1. Your team leader is off sick, and you're asked to help a client in their absence. When your team leader returns the next day, they reprimand you for interfering with their client.

Nondialectical response: _____

_____

Dialectical response: _____

_____

Scenario 2. You read earlier in this book about how acupressure points can help you feel calmer, but you've never heard of this skill before; it sounds strange to you.

Nondialectical response: _____

_____

Dialectical response: _____

_____

Scenario 3. You discover that you and a good friend have very different political views.

Nondialectical response: _____

_____

Dialectical response: _____

_____

POSSIBLE RESPONSES

Scenario 1.

Nondialectical response: *I can never do anything right; they're trying to get rid of me.*

Dialectical response: *I'm feeling very frustrated and confused by my team leader's response. I'm going to ask them why this was a problem.*

Scenario 2.

Nondialectical response: *This is ridiculous. How on earth is something like this going to help me? My problems are way worse than that; this is never going to work.*

Dialectical response: *I'm skeptical that doing this is going to help; however, I'm trying to learn new things to help me with my emotions, so I'll try it and see what happens.*

Scenario 3.

Nondialectical response: *How can I be friends with someone who would vote for that person? I've lost all respect for them. There's no way I can continue this relationship.*

Dialectical response: *My friend and I have completely different political views, and this is difficult for me to accept because my views reflect my values. However, we don't have to agree on everything in order to maintain our friendship.*

You'll see time and again how this theme of balance is important in helping us manage emotions. The next set of skills we'll turn to, known as the DBT states of mind (Linehan 1993), further demonstrates the importance of this balance.

States of Mind

In DBT we refer to the three different ways of thinking about things as our *emotion mind, reasoning mind,* and *wise mind* (Linehan 2014). When we're struggling with a difficult situation, we tend to spend less time in our balanced wise mind and more time in either our emotion or reasoning mind, from which we tend to take more extreme positions. Let's take a closer look at each of these states. Then I'll help you figure out which state you tend to be in most often, so you'll be in a better position to get to that more balanced, wise place.

Emotion Mind

Chanda had a tendency to lash out at others when she was feeling angry or stressed, and she became overwhelmed quite easily, which often led to panic attacks. When it came to making decisions, Chanda often allowed her emotions to cloud her judgment, going with what felt best rather than making a more balanced decision. For example, she had quit more than one job with a knee-jerk emotional reaction, without thinking through the consequences of her decision. It felt right in the moment, so she went with it. Chanda is someone who often acts from her emotion mind.

In emotion mind, our emotions control our behavior, causing us to simply react. This can happen with any emotion: we might lash out at others when we're angry, avoid certain situations when we're anxious, or isolate ourselves when we're feeling sad or ashamed. Allowing our emotions to control us, however, often has negative consequences. For example, lashing out at others will likely push people away, avoiding situations might have us neglecting responsibilities (like going to work) that could get us into trouble and cause us to miss out on living life to the fullest, and isolating ourselves can cause us to feel even more alone. These are just some examples of how emotion mind might get us into trouble, but you can probably think of a lot more! Acting from our emotion mind is typically not in our best interest in the long run, but our emotions can make it difficult for us to really consider the consequences of our actions.

It's important to keep in mind that even though emotions can be painful at times, we need to be able to feel strong feelings, because that allows us to have empathy for others and to stay connected to them. If we haven't experienced pain ourselves, it's difficult to understand the pain of others. Experiencing pain in life also helps us to better appreciate pleasure, which is summed up in this familiar saying: "You can't truly know joy unless you've known suffering."

Emotion mind also includes pleasurable feelings. Think of a time, for example, when you called all of your friends to share good news out of excitement, or when you felt such a deep welling up of love for someone that it brought tears to your eyes. These are examples of acting from emotion mind. We don't want to get rid of emotion mind, rather we want to learn to find a balance with our states of mind.

Write about a time you acted from your emotion mind, allowing emotions to control you.

_____

_____

Reasoning Mind

Kathrine finds herself in her reasoning mind much of the time, really thinking things through before acting, and often not having much awareness of her feelings. When she does notice an emotion, she tends to discount it, pushing it aside to be replaced by logic. For example, a large architect firm recently offered Kathrine a job. She was quite content at her current workplace, but in Kathrine's mind taking the offer made a lot of sense: the pay would be higher and she'd receive good benefits, and the commute would be shorter, so she would even save money on gas. But Kathrine didn't consider the relationships she'd be leaving behind. She had been at her current workplace for many years and had some good friends in the company. She also didn't consider that she really enjoyed the residential projects she worked on there; the new company was known for condominiums and office complexes. In short, Kathrine didn't stop to consider how she felt about the decision; she only considered the logistics.

Being in our reasoning mind means that we're thinking logically or factually, without emotions, or with minimal ones that have no influence on our behavior and are easily disregarded. Most of us use our reasoning mind every day (for example, for writing a to-do list, for planning errands for the day, or for following instructions, such as when trying out a new recipe). You can see that we need this state of mind, and that it's helpful at times, but think about how it might get in our way. Thinking only from our reasoning mind might contribute to difficulties in relationships, because others may feel like we don't understand or accept how they're feeling. Over time this can contribute to rifts in relationships, or a struggle to form strong connections at all.

Write about a time you acted from your reasoning mind, pushing aside or ignoring your emotions and allowing logic or factual thinking to solely dictate your behavior.

_____

_____

While we can see from Chanda's situation that it's not helpful to act only from our emotion mind, Kathrine's situation shows us that it's also not effective to be ruled by our reasoning mind. Ideally, we want to find a balance between these two states and act more often from our wise mind.

Wise Mind

Acting from our wise mind means finding a balance between our emotions and our reasoning and following our intuition, or gut instinct, about what's in our best interest in the long run (Linehan 2014). Wise mind has us considering how we feel, as well as our logical thoughts about a situation, weighing the possible consequences of different actions we might choose and considering our values. In wise mind, we base our decision or behavior on all of these things. In other words, when we're acting from our wise mind, we're *choosing* how we want to act rather than simply *reacting*.

If you struggle at times with regulating emotions, it might feel like you don't have a wise mind—you're out of balance, acting only from emotions (undercontrolled) or only from reasoning (overcontrolled). Rest assured that this isn't the case. Everyone has a wise mind, but it's just more difficult for some people to access it. Look at the following examples and see if you can think of a recent time when you acted from your wise mind.

Chanda was feeling really overwhelmed at her new job, and she could feel her anxiety start to ramp up. She knew she had a tendency to get anxious and annoyed when she hadn't eaten, so she made a point of sitting down at break time and eating a snack. Taking some time for herself helped her to regroup, and when she returned to work she was able to ask her manager some questions that helped her refocus and reduced her stress.

Kathrine had made unhealthy choices for herself in the past because she hadn't stopped to consider how those decisions might make her feel, and she didn't want to make that mistake with this job offer. So, instead of letting her reasoning mind make the decision, she took some time to consider the other parts of this decision as well. Moving away from "just the facts" of her reasoning-minded tendency wasn't easy, but she was able to ask herself what she loved about her current job, and becoming aware that a big part of this was her friendships and her relationships to the homes she created, she realized that the new job wouldn't be such a good fit for her because it wouldn't be as fulfilling.

Here are some other examples of acting from wise mind:

- It's Saturday morning; you don't have to work, but you wake up at your usual 6 a.m. You might reason your way back to sleep (*I don't have anything I need to get up for. My partner is staying in bed, so I may as well stay here too.*), or your emotion mind might keep you in bed (*I don't feel like getting up. It's so comfortable. Who cares if I don't need more sleep; I'm going to stay in bed anyway!*). Instead, you act from your wise mind: *I went to bed early last night and I got enough sleep. If I go back to sleep, I'll probably feel worse when I wake up later, and I have things I could get a head start on now so I can enjoy the day.*

- You have a fight with someone important to you and it's been two days since you've spoken. Emotion mind may have you ruminating out of hurt and anger, thinking things like *They obviously don't care about me, or they would have reached out.* Or reasoning mind may kick in, pushing feelings away and convincing you that *Everything is fine*, perhaps even helping you to forget about the fight. Wise mind, however, acknowledges your feelings, whatever they are, and has you consider the importance of the relationship for you, as well as what's in your best interest and the interest of the relationship. Depending on the answers to these questions, you might decide the wisest action is to not reach out to the person; it's an unhealthy relationship, and you don't want to put excess energy in that direction. Or you might decide that this is an important relationship and it's something you want to direct your attention and emotional energy to.

Think back to a time when you heard that wise voice in the back of your head (whether you listened to it or not!). You know the one, that little voice that reminds you to not just allow your emotions or reasoning to take over, but to make a choice about how to act based on your internal wisdom. This is your wise mind.

Now, write about a time you acted from your wise mind, allowing yourself to feel your emotions but also to consider your reasoning, as well as your values and that internal sense of *knowing*.

_____

_____

It's important to know that emotion mind might sometimes be mistaken for wise mind, because both involve emotions. The key difference is that when you're in emotion mind, your emotions drive your behavior, whereas in wise mind you feel your emotions and *choose* how to act. You'll also know you're in emotion mind when the emotions are intense, and you feel like you're caught up in them. When you're in wise mind, you feel the emotions, but there's a sense of calm or peace, or at least a feeling of being in control, even though the emotions are present (Linehan 2014).

Getting to Know Your States of Mind

In this activity you're going think about what each of these states of mind looks like for you so that your wise mind will be more accessible to you.

Think of a recent difficult situation you experienced. Sticking to the facts as best as you can, write a description of the situation (for example, an argument you had with someone, an urge to do a target behavior, or a crisis happening in your community or in the world).

_____

_____

_____

Considering this situation, make some notes about your emotion mind perspective. (For example, perhaps you noticed strong urges? What thoughts did you notice? Were you judging yourself or others?)

_____

_____

Next, write about your reasoning mind perspective. (Or, if you couldn't reason very well at the time, write what you're thinking about it from that logical, reasoning place now.)

_____

_____

Finally, from your wise mind—including your emotions, reasoning, and values—make some notes about what you _know_ about this situation. (Again, if you didn't have access to this perspective as the situation unfolded, write about what your wise mind tells you now.)

_____

_____

If you found it too difficult to do this exercise retrospectively, you can wait until a difficult situation happens in your life and write about each of these perspectives then.

Now that you're familiar with these states of mind, you might find that you're able to listen to your wise mind more often. But if that doesn't happen right away, don't get discouraged. As you continue to read this book and learn more skills, you'll be able to get to that balanced state more often. It also takes practice, which is what we'll look at next.

Noticing Your State of Mind

You already know that the first step to changing behavior is to increase your awareness of it. You won't be able to get to your wise mind until you first realize that you're not in that balanced place, and that your emotions or reasoning have taken over. To help yourself increase your awareness, regularly ask yourself, *What state of mind am I in right now?* Remembering to do this might be a challenge, as it can be with any new skill. If that's the case, consider writing the question on sticky notes and placing them wherever you'll see them, putting a reminder in your cell phone, or finding ways to incorporate this question into your daily routine. For example, you could ask yourself the question at specific times of the day, such as at mealtimes or when you take a break at work or school. Ideally, you'll do this check-in multiple times every day, because the more often you do it, the more quickly you'll increase your awareness, allowing you to access your wise mind when you want to.

Practice: Getting to Your Wise Self

Like any new skill, it can be difficult to get to your wise mind, especially when you're facing overwhelming emotions. The human tendency is to fall back into old habits and patterns. Here are some ideas to help improve your ability to access your wise mind; give each a try (or come up with your own), find one that resonates with you, and practice it as often as you can so that getting to your wise mind starts to come more naturally, providing emotional relief when things are getting tense.

Mindfulness. The mindfulness of emotions practice from chapter 3 is a good place to start for learning to notice your emotions, thoughts, physical sensations, and urges. Over time you'll learn to just observe these internal experiences rather than react to them. You don't have to do just this practice; any mindfulness practice will help you with this noticing, so be sure to incorporate mindfulness into your daily routine.

Self-talk. How you talk to yourself can influence how you think and feel about things. Bring to mind a recent situation that was painful for you. As you notice the emotion arising within you, focus on saying things to yourself that you would say to your best friend (or partner, or even a pet) if they were feeling this way: *It's okay that you feel like this. You've felt like this before, and you know it doesn't last forever. You'll get through this.* Talking to yourself as you would a friend can reduce the pain you're feeling and help you get to your wise mind.

Ask your wise mind. Ask yourself, *What does my wise mind say right now?* Then listen quietly and see if you get an answer. You might want to close your eyes to do this.

Breathe. Do paced breathing (from chapter 1) or another breathing practice you like to get to your wise mind. You might also pair this with a mantra or saying, such as "Get to" (on the inhale) "wise mind" (on the exhale). Make it fit for you.

In the next section we'll look at some lifestyle choices that can reduce your vulnerability to those intense feeling states and make it more likely that you'll be able to access your wise mind.

Finding Balance in Your Life to Reduce Emotional Reactivity

You can reduce the likelihood of being hijacked by emotions using the acronym STRONG:

Sleep

Treat physical and emotional health problems

Resist using substances

One thing each day to build mastery

Nutrition

Getting exercise

Sleep

Most of us are aware that not getting enough sleep, or sleeping too much, makes it more likely that our emotions will control us. The average adult requires seven to nine hours of sleep each night. The best way to figure out how much sleep you need is to consciously be aware of your daily energy level, as well as things like concentration and memory. If you're not getting the right amount of sleep, you'll be more vulnerable to emotions, putting you at risk for having meltdowns when you get stressed or overwhelmed.

Treat Physical and Emotional Health Problems

It's important to take medications as prescribed and to follow other treatment recommendations for physical and mental health problems. Physical health conditions can contribute to emotion dysregulation, so whether it's something ongoing, such as diabetes or chronic pain, or something shorter term, like having a cold, in order to take care of your mind you need to take care of your body. Most of us are more vulnerable to emotion mind when we're not feeling physically well.

Resist Using Substances

We've already discussed how using drugs or alcohol can be a target behavior for people struggling with emotion dysregulation, but substance use can also be a problem in other ways. You might not be abusing substances or be dependent on them, and you may not even use them regularly, but if at times you turn to drugs or alcohol to help you feel better—to soothe yourself when you have an intense emotion, or to help you relax or feel calmer—this may be a problem. Drugs and alcohol are *mood-altering substances,* and we have no control over how they alter our mood. Drugs and alcohol increase our vulnerability to emotions not just at the time of use, but potentially for days after, so it's important for you to notice how substances affect you over the longer term as well.

One Thing Each Day to Build Mastery

Doing something every day that gives you a sense of being in control, or of mastering your world, also helps to reduce vulnerability to emotions (Linehan 2014). *Building mastery* means doing something that gives you a sense of pride for what you've accomplished, or that provides a sense of fulfillment. This feeling can contribute to an increase in self-respect over time as well. While activities that build mastery will be different for everyone, some examples include exercising, doing volunteer work, or pushing yourself to get something done that you've been procrastinating on.

Nutrition

When we don't eat properly (perhaps eating too much by regularly overeating or binge eating, eating too little by skipping meals or restricting calories, or not eating enough nutritious foods), our body doesn't get the nutrients it needs to perform basic functions, such as breathing, blinking, and moving, never mind what it needs to achieve more complex tasks like concentrating and remembering. Not eating in a balanced way can also affect your mood, making it more likely that you'll be hijacked by emotions. You might be surprised to know that dehydration can also contribute to emotion dysregulation, as signs of dehydration include headaches, confusion, dizziness, and light-headedness, so be sure you're aiming to drink eight glasses of water each day!

It's also important to remember that some foods and beverages contain caffeine, which is a stimulant that can contribute to anxiety, irritability, and poor sleep. Sugar is another substance that can cause emotional instability. By adjusting what you put into your body, you may be able to reduce your vulnerability to emotions (Van Dijk 2021).

Getting Exercise

Exercise can help us manage our emotions more effectively. Some studies have shown that cardiovascular exercise (that which gets your heart rate going) is just as effective at reducing depression as antidepressant medication. Even if you don't suffer from depression, exercise can help you manage your emotions in healthier ways. And of course, you don't have to do cardio exercise; my philosophy is anything more than what you're doing now will be beneficial! Go for a stroll, try some yoga, take up swimming. The key is to get your body moving.

Getting STRONG

Answer the following questions to help you decide which of the STRONG skills you want to work on in order to reduce your vulnerability to emotion mind.

Sleep

Approximately how many hours of sleep do you get each night? _____

Do you generally feel rested when you wake up? _____

Do you usually take a nap during the day? If so, for how long? _____

After you nap, do you usually feel better or worse? _____

Do you ingest substances that could be interfering with your ability to get good sleep, such as caffeine or other stimulants (think coffee, tea, energy drinks, caffeine pills, diet pills)?

_____

Do you use your phone or other screens right up until bedtime? _____

Based on your answers, and keeping in mind that too much or too little sleep can leave you feeling lethargic and sluggish, do you need to increase or decrease the amount of time you're sleeping?

_____

If you've identified sleep as an area to work on, what's one small step you can take to start working toward that goal? (For example, if you need more sleep, you could set a goal to go to bed a half hour earlier tonight, then work your way up to an hour, or you might need to reduce or eliminate caffeine to help you sleep better. Keep in mind that technology should be turned off at least thirty minutes before bedtime to improve sleep.)

_____

_____

_____

Treat Physical and Emotional Health Problems

Do you have a physical or mental health problem that requires medication or other treatment? If so, do you follow your doctor's directions for treatment?

_____

If you've identified this as an area to work on, what's one small step you can take to start working toward that goal? (For example, you could learn more about your illness to understand why the medication or treatment is necessary.)

_____

_____

_____

Resist Using Substances

Do you currently drink alcohol or use drugs? If so, what, and how often?

_____

Does your use cause problems for you at work, at school, in relationships, or in any other aspect of your life?

_____

Has anyone ever told you that your substance use is a problem? _____

When you're using drugs or alcohol, do you tend to make poor decisions or do things that you later regret?

_____

Do you find yourself turning to drugs or alcohol to deal with your emotions?

_____

If you've identified this as an area to work on, what's one small step you can take to start working toward that goal? (For example, if alcohol is a problem, you could set a goal to drink only one night each week instead of two and decrease your consumption from there. If you don't think this is a problem you can handle on your own, you might set a goal to look into getting help.)

_____

_____

_____

One Thing Each Day to Build Mastery

Remembering that building mastery is about doing things that help you feel fulfilled, productive, and like you're in control of your world, how often do you do something that builds mastery for you?

_____

List at least three things that you do regularly to build mastery.

_____

If you've identified this as an area to work on, what's one small step you can take to start working toward that goal? (For example, you might make a list of activities you used to do that gave you this feeling, or other activities you can try.)

_____

_____

_____

Nutrition

Do you eat three meals as well as some snacks each day? _____

Do your meals and snacks tend to be healthy? _____

Do you find yourself eating just because you have an urge to—maybe out of boredom or because you're feeling a painful emotion?

_____

Do you find yourself not eating at times so you can lose weight or feel more in control?

_____

How much caffeine do you ingest each day? _____

How many glasses of water do you drink each day? _____

Sometimes people develop problems with eating for which they need to seek professional help. If you feel you have an eating problem that you're unable to manage on your own, please speak to your family doctor or other professional. If this isn't the case, but you've identified eating as an area to work on, what's one small step you can take to start working toward that goal? (For example, if you currently eat only one meal a day, you could set a goal to eat something small for breakfast and increase your consumption from there.)

_____

_____

_____

Getting Exercise

Do you currently do any type of exercise? If so, how often and for how long?

_____

Keep in mind that if you have any kind of health problem, you'll want to check with your doctor before you start an exercise routine. If you've identified exercise as an area to work on, what's one small step you can take to start working toward that goal? (For example, if you currently exercise twice a week for fifteen minutes, you could increase this to three times a week and work your way up to more.)

_____

_____

_____

It can be easy to take on too much at once, so if you've identified more than one STRONG skill to work on, take some time now to decide which area you'll work on first. You can always work on the others later. Which STRONG skill are you starting with?

_____

Rescue Skill: Wise Mind Shortcut

It typically takes practice to learn how to access your wise mind, but I've found this shortcut helpful. Think of a person who represents the wise mind perspective for you. Then, when you're in a difficult situation, you can simply bring this individual to mind to help you get to a more balanced, wise-minded perspective by asking yourself what they would do.

Who represents wise mind for you? (It could be someone in your personal life, or it could be a famous person or fictional character):

_____

This shortcut can be especially effective if you tie it in with some of the skills you learned earlier for managing emotions. For example, as you (take your pick) do a forward bend, stick your face in cold water, do paced breathing, count your breaths, do progressive muscle relaxation, massage an acupressure point (or do something else that helps you slow your emotions down), ask yourself, _What would [your wise-minded person] do or say right now?_ Then, of course, do your best to act on your wise mind's advice!

Wrapping Up

In this chapter you learned about the importance of taking a dialectical perspective, and how this helps with emotion regulation. You also learned about the three states of mind we all have, and how to access your wise mind to help you find a more balanced way of responding. And we looked at lifestyle changes you can make to reduce your vulnerability to emotions using the STRONG acronym. In the next chapter we'll look at DBT skills involving acceptance that will help reduce the intensity of the emotions you're experiencing.

Remember, the more you practice the skills you're learning outside of problematic situations, the more you'll be able to access them when things get difficult. Firefighters train and drill over and over again so that when a crisis happens, they know exactly what to do. They've trained so well that muscle memory takes over and they don't need to stop and think about what to do; they just go through the steps naturally. Learning and practicing emotion regulation skills is no different, so practice, practice, practice outside of problematic situations, and over time these skills will become more like a reflex.

CHAPTER 6

Reducing Emotional Pain

In the last chapter we looked at dialectics as a way to help us take a more balanced perspective and to access wise mind. In this chapter we'll look at three skills that will help prevent emotions from intensifying, reduce the pain if it's already intense, and improve your ability to get to (or stay in) your wise mind: nonjudgmental stance, reality acceptance, and self-validation. These skills are very much intertwined with one another and connected to mindfulness. They can also be hard to wrap your head around, so to help humanize the concepts we'll reflect on Joachim's story throughout the chapter.

Joachim is forty-three years old and successful in his career. He's married with two teenagers, and though he loves his partner, they fight a lot—about everything, but especially about how they parent. Joachim is quick to anger and yells a lot; he's been working on this, but his partner tells him regularly he's not doing enough, and he feels like he's never good enough. Joachim often feels anxious and stressed, worrying about when the next argument will happen and trying to get the kids to listen to him hoping to prevent it. It's exhausting. He feels like he's on guard all the time, and he experiences a lot of shame when he finds himself judging his partner and kids. *What kind of person does that?*

Many of the skills we've covered in this workbook could help Joachim reduce his emotional pain, but let's look at the three skills mentioned above.

Nonjudgmental Stance

How often do you find yourself judging—people, situations, the weather, and so on—either out loud or just to yourself? Or maybe you're harder on yourself than others, and you regularly beat yourself up as being "stupid" or "lazy," or you remind yourself of all the things you "should" or "shouldn't" have done. Does this sound familiar? When we judge we tend to trigger extra emotional pain for ourselves, which is why the nonjudgmental stance is such an important skill. Let's start by looking at what we mean with that word "judgment."

What Is a Judgment?

Think of a judgment as negative or positive shorthand we attach to something or someone. For example, when Joachim's partner does something he doesn't agree with, and Joachim says his partner is a "bad parent," he's judging. "Bad" is a shorthand label that doesn't provide any helpful information. If Joachim's partner wants to make changes so they're no longer a "bad" parent, they're not actually going to know how based on that label. And, this judgment is not only likely to cause hurt feelings in Joachim's partner, but also to increase Joachim's emotions, because negative judgments contribute to emotional pain, often preventing us from acting effectively. If Joachim said instead, "I don't like it when you do that," this would be an expression of emotion rather than judgment. Emotions are not judgments and are actually part of a nonjudgmental statement, which we'll come back to shortly.

Figuring out what's a judgment and what's not can be difficult, so before we go any further, let's do an exercise to practice this discernment.

Identifying Judgments

Read each of the following statements and circle whether you think it's a judgment or a nonjudgment. The answers are at the end of the exercise.

1.	I made a stupid mistake at work today.	Judgment	Nonjudgment
2.	I'm an idiot for losing my temper.	Judgment	Nonjudgment
3.	I feel ashamed for speaking to my partner the way I did.	Judgment	Nonjudgment
4.	I love this movie!	Judgment	Nonjudgment
5.	I'm disappointed that I won't get to go on vacation this year.	Judgment	Nonjudgment
6.	I can't watch the news anymore because it makes me so mad that everything in the world is going to shit.	Judgment	Nonjudgment
7.	The sunset this evening was beautiful.	Judgment	Nonjudgment
8.	When I was driving home today, I saw someone driving really dangerously. It scared me and made me angry.	Judgment	Nonjudgment
9.	It's ridiculous that people can get away with treating other people so badly.	Judgment	Nonjudgment
10.	I hate that there's still so much inequality in the world.	Judgment	Nonjudgment

Answers

1.   The word "stupid" is a judgment.

2.   The word "idiot" is a judgment.

3.   Feeling "ashamed" is an emotion (nonjudgment).

4.   "Loving" something is an emotion (nonjudgment).

5.   "Disappointment" is an emotion (nonjudgment).

6.   "Everything…is going to shit" is judgmental language.

7.   "Beautiful" is a judgment.

8.   "Dangerous" is an evaluation, not a judgment (more on this shortly), and "scared" and "angry" are emotions, so also nonjudgmental.

9.   "Ridiculous" and "badly" are both judgments.

10. "I hate" is an emotion, so nonjudgmental, and it is a fact that there is inequality in the world, so this is an evaluation (nonjudgmental).

How did you do? If you struggled, you're not alone! By the end of this chapter, and with practice, you'll be better able to identify judgments and nonjudgments. Let's examine how being less judgmental will help you manage emotions more effectively.

The Effects of Judgments on Emotions

Typically, a painful emotion sparks our judging: for example, we feel irritated or annoyed about something, causing us to judge. The judgment increases the intensity of our emotion, leading to more judgment, and causing more pain. When you add judgments, even low-level anger can turn into full-on rage.

Can you relate to this cycle? Think of a recent time when you felt "bothered," "frustrated," or "annoyed"—with yourself, someone else, or a situation (for example, being stuck in traffic, seeing a coworker shirking their responsibilities, or hearing about another man-made disaster in the world). Have a look at the following example, then write about your own experience.

Describe the situation (sticking to just the facts).

My coworker just walked into my office without knocking and interrupted me while I was on a call.

What were your initial feelings toward the situation or person?

Surprised and annoyed.

What were your judgmental thoughts?

What the hell is the matter with them? That was so rude!

How did your emotions change as a result of the judgments? (Did the emotional intensity increase, decrease, or stay the same? Were there additional emotions that joined the original ones?)

My emotions definitely increased. I went from surprised and annoyed to angry very quickly.

Now it's your turn.

Describe the situation (sticking to just the facts).

_____

_____

What were your initial feelings toward the situation or person?

_____

What were your judgmental thoughts?

_____

_____

How did your emotions change as a result of the judgments? (Did the emotional intensity increase, decrease, or stay the same? Were there additional emotions that joined the original ones?)

_____

_____

What was it like for you to write about your experience? Do you see this cycle contributing to your emotional intensity at times?

_____

_____

_____

Not everyone sees this connection immediately, but pretty much everyone I work with gets stuck in this vicious cycle at times. (I admit I get stuck there myself sometimes!) Most people will benefit from practicing the skill of nonjudgmental stance, but if you're not sure yet, the Monitoring Judgments Worksheet can help you determine if it's a skill you should be paying more attention to. I included a sample for you, and you can download additional copies at this book's website: http://www.newharbinger.com/49647.

Monitoring Judgments Worksheet

Situation	Emotion(s)	Judgment	"Extra" Emotion	Outcome
Argued with my partner because they wouldn't drive the kids to school.	Hurt, angry	They should want to help out.	More anger	No resolution to argument; we just haven't talked about it.
Sitting on the couch, watching TV by myself.	Depressed, lonely	There must be something wrong with me. I shouldn't feel like this.	Anger toward myself, even more sadness	Feel worse than before; end up drinking to avoid my feelings.
My partner decided to go mountain biking this weekend instead of spending time with me.	Hurt, sad, lonely	What a jerk. They clearly love mountain biking more than they love me.	Anger, anxiety	I withdrew from my partner, ignoring their calls at times, and ended up worrying about our relationship.
Driving home I got stuck in traffic.	Annoyed, impatient	People are stupid. They don't know how to drive.	More anger	I was just sitting in my car, all by myself, feeling really angry!
Watching the news.	Sad, worried	The human race sucks. We ruin everything, and we can't even treat each other with kindness.	Anger, hopelessness, despair	I got so angry and felt hopeless and despairing; started to cry; ended up eating and mindlessly watching TV before going to bed early.

Monitoring Judgments Worksheet

Situation	Emotion(s)	Judgment	"Extra" Emotion	Outcome

I suggest you complete this worksheet for one week, to help you get a more objective perspective on whether judgments are an issue for you. Often people become more aware of their judgmental language once they start learning about the effects judgments can have on emotions, so you might naturally find yourself catching your judgments; if not, pay attention to the times when the level of your emotions (especially anger emotions) seem higher than what's warranted by the situation. This is generally a reliable sign that you're judging. If judgments aren't a problem for you…count yourself lucky and move on to the next skill. If you find that judgments *are* an issue, you're not alone! Now you know what you're dealing with, and you can start practicing the nonjudgmental stance skill.

This worksheet can also help you identify patterns, if you don't know them already. For example, are there certain situations in which you tend to be more judgmental, or certain people you tend to be harder on? Tracking how often a behavior happens can actually help us change that behavior, so that's another way this worksheet might be helpful!

Judgments vs. Evaluations

Keep in mind that we're not trying to eliminate judgments altogether. That's likely not possible, nor is it necessary, because not every judgment is problematic from an emotional perspective. It's also important to know that there are, of course, times when we need to judge, but I label these "necessary judgments" as "evaluations." Consider these examples:

- Discerning if a situation is *safe* or *unsafe*

- Deciding if a relationship is *satisfying* or *healthy*

- Determining whether we've made a mistake or acted according to our values

The judgments we want to work on reducing with the nonjudgmental stance, therefore, are the unnecessary judgments that trigger emotional pain.

Self-Judgments

I mentioned earlier that some of us judge ourselves more harshly and more often than we judge others. Does this sound like you? Do you often say things to yourself like *There's something wrong with me?* Do you judge yourself as "stupid" or an "idiot" (or worse!) when you make a mistake? Or maybe you "should" yourself, as in *I should have…* Over time judgmental self-talk contributes to lower self-esteem and can intensify feelings of anger, shame, depression, and anxiety. Think of your self-judgment as you bullying yourself. If you wouldn't say something to someone you care about, it's not okay to say it to yourself.

It tends to be more difficult to notice self-judgments, because they're often very ingrained in us and therefore usually happen automatically. Also, you might not say them out loud, which makes them less noticeable. So, if you do beat yourself up a lot, I recommend that you get comfortable using the nonjudgmental stance with other judgments first. Practicing being nonjudgmental toward other people or situations will help you get more comfortable with this difficult skill so that, over time, you'll be more capable of applying a nonjudgmental attitude to yourself.

A final word about judgments before we look at how to be nonjudgmental: it's important to recognize that judgments are part of how many of us grew up. Generally, judgments are so commonplace in society that we often don't even realize that we're judging. For example, we grow up hearing how "good" or "bad" we are, that something is "right" or "wrong," that we "should" or "shouldn't" do things, and so on. Because we typically hear judgmental messages so frequently and from such a young age, we usually can't help but use this language ourselves. So don't judge yourself for judging (Linehan 2014)! Instead, consider what you're going to do about it.

How to Be Nonjudgmental

As with any behavior we're trying to change, the first step is to become aware of the behavior. (Mindfulness will help with that!) You may not always realize you're judging, but you may notice emotions (frequently anger emotions) suddenly intensifying, which is often an indication that you're judging. So take a close look at your thoughts when it seems like your emotions seem overly intense, and see if you can identify the judgments that are enhancing these emotions.

Once you become aware of a judgment, see if you can just let it go. There are many ways you might do this. For example, you can notice the judgment, take a deep breath, and remind yourself to think dialectically; or you can nonjudgmentally remind yourself that the person's behavior doesn't concern you. These tactics are good options for engaging the nonjudgmental stance when you're not emotionally invested in a situation. For example, you see someone outside dressed inappropriately for the weather and think, *They're weird.* This is a judgment, but because it doesn't affect you, you can easily let it go. When you become aware of a judgment that you can't let go of, the next step is to turn it into a nonjudgmental statement.

Being nonjudgmental is *not* about turning a negative into a positive. First, you likely wouldn't believe it. For example, if Joachim regularly tells himself *I'm a bad parent,* he's probably not going to believe he's a good parent if he simply changes this statement to *I'm a good parent.* Second, if we judge something in a positive way, that positive can turn into a negative judgment. If Joachim tells himself he's a good parent, does that mean the next time he yells at his kids he's back to being a bad parent?

When turning a judgment into a nonjudgment, it's important to look at two things. First, what are you really trying to say? Remember, a judgment is usually a shorthand label, so get rid of it and stick to the facts—that is, the long version. Second, what's the emotion? Being nonjudgmental isn't about stuffing your emotions; it's really about being assertive. So, if we return to Joachim's judgment of *I'm a bad parent* and apply these two concepts, we might end up with something like *I feel disappointed in myself for yelling at the kids.* Being nonjudgmental will not take your emotion away, but it will reduce the extra emotions you're experiencing (or prevent you from adding more in the first place), which will help you to access your wise mind.

What Nonjudgmental Stance Isn't

When learning to be nonjudgmental, some people get stuck in the trap of making excuses. Let's say your partner hasn't been spending a lot of time with you recently, and you're feeling hurt and lonely. You might try to be nonjudgmental about this, saying to yourself, *I know they're working a lot of hours right now, so we're not getting as much time together as we normally would.* While this might be true—in which case this might be a compassionate stance to take with them—this isn't nonjudgmental stance. The implication of excusing or rationalizing behavior is that you *shouldn't* be feeling what you're feeling, and so you end up judging yourself for your emotions, which is likely going to lead to more emotions! Remember, the goal is to let go of the judgment if you can; and if not, then go for neutral. So rather than trying to think of the reasons why your partner isn't spending much time with you right now, one way to rephrase this judgment is, *My partner isn't spending as much time with me as I'd like, and I feel hurt and lonely.* Facts of the situation, and feelings.

Now it's your turn. Return to the earlier situation you wrote about in which you found yourself judging, and answer these questions to help you create a nonjudgmental statement.

Describe the situation and your judgmental thoughts.

_____

_____

_____

_____

Now state the facts of the situation.

_____

_____

What are your emotions?

_____

Now combine these to make your nonjudgmental statement.

_____

_____

_____

Hopefully you're starting to see that being nonjudgmental can help to reduce the intensity of emotions, which will make them more manageable. As you practice this skill, however, you might become aware of how much other people are judging; if this happens, don't judge them for judging either! I encourage you to share these skills with others. You can certainly teach your loved ones about being more mindful of their judgments, if they're open to making these changes. If they're not, remember that you can't change others, so focus on you.

A final word on judgments (and all the skills you're learning): you get to choose when you use skills. If you want to go on that rant and judge, go for it…as long as you're aware of what you're doing, and that you're increasing the emotions you're experiencing. Let's face it, sometimes we choose to do what's easiest (and familiar!), rather than what we know would be more effective. Over time, as being nonjudgmental starts to come more naturally, you'll probably find that you choose to judge and inflame your emotions less often.

Now we have some other, related skills to get to, starting with reality acceptance.

Reality Acceptance

Let me first clarify that the "acceptance" in "reality acceptance" doesn't mean *approving of, liking,* or *being okay with* something (Linehan 2003c) but is just about acknowledging reality as it is. Because this skill involves being nonjudgmental, you're already working on acceptance by practicing the skill you just learned. (And for that matter, since being nonjudgmental and accepting is part of being mindful, you've already been working on both of these skills!) Nonetheless, accepting reality is a broader skill in which we focus on bringing a more accepting attitude to whatever past or present reality we've been fighting.

How Acceptance Helps

To give you a sense of how this skill will be helpful, let's do an exercise.

Think of a situation in your life that you've accepted. It could be something from the past (like a traumatic event or not getting a job you wanted), or something in the present (such as a struggle with your kids or dealing with the loss of a relationship). Whatever the situation, while you may have fought it when it first happened, you've been able to accept it. Briefly describe the situation.

_____

_____

Now recall what it was like when that situation first happened and compare that to how you experience the situation now that you've accepted it. What changed for you once you got to acceptance? How did acceptance make a difference? Or did it?

_____

_____

People often say that accepting a situation led to a sense of relief, as if a weight had been lifted. They may feel like the situation has less power over them, they think about it less often, and when they do think about it, there's less pain, more clarity, and a sense of peace or calm. Sometimes people feel like they're more able to *let go* or *move on*. Hopefully you can see how accepting reality will help reduce emotional pain, making it less likely that you'll get stuck in those moments of emotional hijack.

Fighting Reality vs. Accepting Reality

Now that you have a sense of how this skill will help, let's look more closely at what it is. Accepting reality is the opposite of *fighting reality*. Do you notice your thoughts turn to *Why me? It's not fair* or *It shouldn't be this way* in challenging situations? These thoughts are a form of fighting reality; essentially, you're judging reality. Remember, accepting reality doesn't mean you're *okay with* the situation, or that you *like things as they are,* but when you fight reality like this, you're creating extra emotional pain for yourself.

Activity: What Are You Not Accepting?

Now it's your turn to think about how accepting reality applies to you. What realities are you fighting? Make a list of the things you need to accept. Examples might include a specific choice you made that you're now regretting, a physical or mental health diagnosis or addiction you're struggling with, the fact that your partner regularly leaves their shoes in front of the door, or really anything that you find yourself fighting on a regular basis! (If you need more room, grab another piece of paper and keep writing!)

_____

_____

_____

_____

_____

Examining what fighting reality (for example, lashing out at others, using substances, sleeping too much, shopping, or other means of avoiding reality) looks like for you, and how this contributes to emotion dysregulation, can also help motivate you to use this skill. How are you fighting these realities?

_____

_____

_____

Steps to Reality Acceptance

Now that you know what realities you need to work on accepting, and how doing so will help you regulate your emotions, here are the steps to help you get there.

Step 1: Choose what you're going to work on accepting. Don't start with the most difficult situation in your life! Choose something less painful to start with, and then work your way up to the more painful situations. If it seems impossible right now to choose one, or if you find yourself not willing to work on accepting any of the situations on your list, find something else (like the weather, or the line at the coffee shop). Now make this commitment to yourself: *As of right now, I'm going to work on accepting* _____.

Step 2: Notice when you're fighting that reality. Write down some of the fighting reality thoughts you notice (for example, *It's not fair, It's not right, It shouldn't be this way,* or *This is stupid*).

_____

_____

Step 3: Remind yourself of why you want to accept this reality. (For example, *I know that accepting will help me spend less energy on the situation. It will help me let go and feel more at peace.*) Change your fighting reality self-talk to accepting reality.

　　Then repeat steps 2 and 3 over and over and over again. Notice when you're fighting reality and turn your mind back to acceptance. I call this the "internal argument," and it's a normal part of the process of accepting. You will waffle back and forth!

It can be helpful to write out some accepting statements you can read to yourself when you fall back into fighting reality. Reading them to yourself will gradually help you shift your thinking to acknowledging that this is how it is. Here are some of Joachim's statements that help him accept moments when he yells at his kids:

- The past is in the past. I can't go back and change it.

- I want to work on accepting my past so it doesn't continue to limit my future.

- It is what it is, and I'm doing everything in my power to change my behavior.

Now it's your turn. Thinking of that situation you chose to start working on accepting, write some statements that will help you to stop fighting and instead acknowledge reality as it is:

- _____

- _____

- _____

- _____

　　Keep this list with you so you can read these statements when fighting reality thoughts arise (what I refer to as "reactive" practice), and also read them regularly just for the sake of practicing, to strengthen this new way of thinking (what I call "proactive" practice).

　　Before we move on from reality acceptance, I want to emphasize this: acceptance means you're acknowledging reality. If you choose to accept something, it doesn't mean you're being passive or giving up on trying to change it. In fact, the next step will often be deciding if there's something you can do about it, and at this juncture many other skills will come into play. So don't let the idea that acceptance equates with giving up get in the way of you choosing to accept something.

So far, we've looked at practicing the nonjudgmental stance and reality acceptance with specific situations or people (including ourselves). In this final section we're going to look at how we can also use these skills to more directly address our emotions.

Self-Validation

Have you ever noticed that you judge yourself for feeling certain emotions? Many of us have at least one emotion that we struggle with in this way, and some people have difficulty with many different emotions. This form of judgment is *self-invalidation*. To help you understand the importance of self-validation, let's first look at the two types of emotions we experience: primary and secondary emotions.

Primary and Secondary Emotions

Most primary emotions we experience are in response to our interpretation of an event or situation (this could be an external event, like having a fight with your partner, or an internal event, such as a thought, memory, or physical sensation). I like to think of a *primary emotion* as a first responder because it's the first to show up on the scene.

A *secondary emotion* arises in response to a primary emotion; it's *how we feel about our feelings* (Linehan 1993). In other words, we interpret a situation or event in a certain way, triggering a primary emotion, and if we then have thoughts about how we feel (often based on the messages we've received about emotions from our family, peers, or society in general), secondary emotions arise. So, Joachim has a fight with his partner and feels angry in response to his interpretation of something his partner said (primary emotion). If Joachim learned that anger is "bad," he might think to himself, *I shouldn't be angry*, or *I'm a bad person for feeling angry*. This triggers a secondary emotion: Joachim may feel angry at himself, or he may feel guilt or shame for feeling angry. So you can see how we increase our emotional pain by judging ourselves for how we feel.

What emotions are you not allowed to feel? Do you tell yourself to *calm down*, that you *have nothing to feel sad about*, or that you *shouldn't be angry*? Trying to push away or avoid feelings is inherently judgmental; so, while you might not be judging consciously, stuffing or bottling emotions up is also invalidation. Considering the emotions we discussed in chapter 4 (anger, fear, sadness, guilt, shame, envy, jealousy, disgust, love, and happiness), write the names of the emotions you think you tend to judge yourself for feeling:

_____   _____

_____   _____

If you're struggling in these blanks, you might find it helpful to look back at some of the behavioral analyses you've completed (chapter 1); they may provide insights.

Once you've identified at least one emotion you need to work on validating, you can also consider where your beliefs about this emotion come from: Was it not okay in your family to feel this way? Or perhaps you were bullied in school, and you learned that showing any kind of pain was "weak." For some people pleasurable emotions can also be difficult to bear, perhaps having received messages that they were "too hyper" when they were excited or joyful, or their expressions of love and affection made others uncomfortable. This isn't about blaming your family, but about understanding where your beliefs about emotions come from, which can help you be more accepting of them.

Hopefully you're starting to see how, when you invalidate yourself (*judge* or refuse to accept your emotions), you create more emotional pain for yourself in the form of secondary emotions. Remember, accepting something doesn't mean you like it, it just means you're acknowledging it. When you acknowledge your primary emotion, the feeling typically won't go away, but it won't turn into something stronger, and that means you'll be more able to get to your wise mind to determine if there's something you can do to help reduce the pain.

How to Validate Your Emotions

So, how do you stop judging your emotions? The first step, of course, is to increase your awareness. If you don't know how you think and feel about your emotions, you won't be able to change your response. Mindfulness, such as the mindfulness of emotions practice we did in chapter 3, will help with this. The next step is to start changing your self-talk. Here are three ways to validate your emotions (Van Dijk 2012).

1. **Acknowledging.** The most basic form of self-validating is acknowledging the presence of the primary emotion: for example, "I feel _____." By simply labeling the emotion accurately, you're validating it.

2. **Allowing.** Another form of self-validating is allowing yourself, or giving yourself permission, to feel the emotion: for example, "It's okay that I feel _____." You're not saying "It's okay" in the sense that you like it or want it to hang around, you're just noting that you're allowed to feel it.

3. **Understanding.** The third and most difficult form of self-validating is saying, "It makes sense that I feel _____." You might be able to understand the emotion based on past experience (for example, "It makes sense that I feel anxious when I'm meeting new people, because I was bullied when I was a kid"), or based on the present (for example, "It makes sense that I feel anxious about public speaking, because it's not something I'm used to doing").

We can't always understand why we feel the way we do, but even if we can't understand our emotion, we can still validate it by either acknowledging its presence or allowing it. Now let's get you working on validating your emotions.

Creating Self-Validating Statements

Hopefully you've been able to identify which emotions you need to work on validating. As I mentioned before, you don't want to overwhelm yourself by taking on everything at once. If you've identified more than one emotion you judge yourself for feeling, choose just one to start with. You can always come back and work on the others later. In the space provided, write out some statements to validate your emotion. I've provided some examples from Joachim; feel free to use these if they resonate for you, or to tweak them to make them fit your emotion.

Emotion: Anger

- I feel angry.

- Anger is a normal human emotion that we all feel at times, so it's okay that I feel this way.

- I'm feeling angry; it's uncomfortable, but it is what it is.

- It makes sense that I'm feeling angry, because I just had a fight with my partner.

- I'm feeling angry right now, but that doesn't mean anything about me as a person.

- It makes sense that I have anger problems because of the environment I grew up in.

Emotion: _____

- _____

- _____

- _____

- _____

And you probably know the drill by now: practice, practice, practice. Read these statements to yourself reactively, when you hear the judgments arise in response to that painful feeling, and proactively, just for the sake of practicing changing your self-talk. As with any new skill, it will likely be challenging when you first start trying to take a nonjudgmental, accepting, or validating stance. Don't forget to bring in other skills (sticking your face in cold water, forward bend, and so on) to help when you need to regulate your emotions.

A CAUTION ABOUT VALIDATING GUILT AND SHAME

If you noted that you need to work on validating guilt and shame, I urge you to look more closely at these two emotions, perhaps revisiting chapter 4 where we looked at each of them in detail, and to identify whether or not your guilt and shame are primary emotions. While it's possible that they are primary emotions, guilt and shame often show up as secondary emotions; we feel them when we judge ourselves for feeling something else. If, for example, you judge yourself as "bad," or if you think *This is wrong, I shouldn't feel this way* when you're feeling angry at someone, you'll probably feel shame (if you're judging yourself) or guilt (if you're judging the feeling). If instead you can *accept* that you're feeling angry, neither of these secondary emotions will arise. Validating a secondary emotion won't do any harm, but it's also not going to get you very far. Validating the primary emotion will ensure that you don't experience secondary emotions.

Rescue Skill: Half Smile

Have you heard the saying, "Sometimes your joy is the source of your smile, but sometimes your smile is the source of your joy"? Research has shown that changing our facial expression can influence our mood (Ekman and Davidson 1993). The idea behind the half smile (Linehan 2014) is that by slightly turning the corners of our mouth up—try for less than the *Mona Lisa*—we can improve our sense of well-being. The half smile is a very slight smile—so slight that if you're looking at yourself in a mirror you might not be able to see it, but you *feel* it. Let me clarify that this isn't a fake smile, which creates tension in the muscles in our face that *reduces* our sense of well-being. If you're struggling to find the balance with this expression, bite down on a pen; doing so will turn the corners of your mouth up slightly. Give the half smile a try the next time you notice emotional pain arising. Try it with different emotions at different times.

Wrapping Up

In this chapter you learned some skills to help you get to a more accepting place: nonjudgmental stance will help you change the language you're using in order to be more accepting; reality acceptance to help you be more generally accepting of yourself, others, and situations; and self-validation to help you be more accepting of your emotions. These skills will help you when you're in a crisis situation and emotions are intensifying. And, of course, since they'll help keep your emotions at a more manageable level, you'll experience fewer crises.

In the next chapter we'll look at more skills to help reduce your emotional pain, thereby decreasing the frequency of those emotional highjacks. Remember to take your time as you move through this workbook, ensuring that you understand the skills you're learning, that you're putting them into practice, and even that you're picking and choosing the ones that are most important for you to focus on in your own life right now. Keep practicing, and when you're ready to move on, turn the page.

CHAPTER 7

Changing Your Emotions

In the last chapter you learned how to manage your emotions through the acceptance-based skills of being nonjudgmental, accepting reality, and self-validation. While it's important to be able to accept your experience to prevent extra emotions from arising (or to calm the ones that are already there), there are also times when you'll want to be able to draw on skills to change your emotions and your situation. You've learned some of these change-oriented skills already (such as changing your body's chemistry and taking a more balanced perspective), and in this chapter you'll learn two more: opposite to emotion action and being effective.

Opposite to Emotion Action

While every emotion serves a purpose, and we're therefore not trying to stuff or ignore them, we often have emotions that we want to reduce in intensity. The problem is that, as we like to say in DBT, *emotions love themselves* (Linehan 2000), and they keep us feeding them by creating urges that, when we act on them, make the emotion stronger. Think about a time this has happened to you: You feel anxious about going to a social event, so you don't go, but that avoidance increases your anxiety the next time you're invited to an event. Or you feel sad, and you follow the urge to isolate yourself, which causes you to feel more down.

But you've probably also had times when you didn't do what the emotion was telling you to do: You felt the anxiety and went to the event anyway, your anxiety dissipated, and you even enjoyed yourself! Or you felt sad but reached out to someone and found that having company made you feel better. Here you're going to learn how to use this skill in a conscious way to reduce the likelihood of your emotions hijacking you.

How to Act Opposite to Your Emotion

First, you need to decide if this skill fits the situation you're facing. Acting opposite is a skill you use when you want to reduce the intensity of your emotion; if that's not your goal (even if it's someone else's goal for you!), acting opposite won't work. Sometimes you'll want to reduce an emotion because it's painful or because you know it may lead to problematic behavior. Sometimes you might recognize that an emotion is stronger than what's warranted by the situation (especially if you're a more highly sensitive person), and you want to bring the emotion down. Sometimes, by the way, you might be okay with the emotion, or even get a sense of satisfaction out of it, but your wise mind recognizes that staying there isn't effective, and the emotion is likely to get in your way (for example, when you're feeling angry with someone). These are all examples of moments when acting opposite to your emotion is likely to be helpful.

Before you can practice this skill you need to be able to name your emotions accurately. If that skill is still a work in progress for you, I suggest returning to chapter 4 and continuing to work on it (in conjunction with other skills like mindfulness) until you're more comfortable with it. Otherwise, if you feel ready to practice acting opposite to your emotion, follow these four steps.

Step 1: Identify the emotion and the urge associated with it. What's the emotion telling you to do?

Step 2: Validate the emotion. Acknowledge it by naming it, allow it by giving yourself permission to feel it, or understand it by giving it context.

Step 3: Ask yourself if the emotion is justified. This step can be tricky, and it's important to remember that, regardless of whether or not the emotion is justified, it's always *valid*, so you must validate the emotion first! But if you recall the Emotion Reference Sheets in chapter 4, all emotions serve a purpose, and sometimes we feel emotions when they're not justified by the situation we're facing. I included this concept in a chart we'll look at shortly to help you with this skill.

Step 4: If the emotion is justified, you'll often want to do what the emotion is telling you to do—remember, our emotions are messengers! If you're crossing the road and a car comes racing toward you, fear will cause you to jump out of harm's way; in this situation fear is justified (Your life is at risk!), so do what the emotion is telling you to do. Similarly, if you're facing discrimination at work, anger will motivate you to try to make changes; your anger is justified, so you want to do what the emotion is telling you to do (although we'll look more closely at anger shortly, since it isn't usually this straightforward).

When the emotion *isn't* justified, doing the opposite of what the emotion is urging you to do will help reduce the intensity of the emotion. The following chart, which includes some of the common urges associated with our emotions and suggestions for acting opposite, can help you identify if your emotion is justified.

Emotion	When Is It Justified?	Urge	How to Act Opposite
Anger	When there's something blocking us from reaching a goal. When we or someone we care about is being attacked, threatened, insulted, or hurt.	Lash out—attack someone or something, physically or verbally. Judge the person or situation you're angry with.	Be respectful or civil; if this is too difficult, gently avoid the person or the situation. Change judgments to nonjudgmental, accepting thoughts.
Sadness	When things aren't the way we expected them to be or when we've experienced a loss.	Disconnect from others, isolate yourself. Stop doing your regular activities.	Reach out and connect with others. Reengage in your usual activities.
Fear or Anxiety	When there is a threat to our safety or well-being or to that of someone we care about.	Avoid what's causing the fear or anxiety. Escape or leave the situation causing fear or anxiety.	Approach the situation or person causing the fear or anxiety. Stay in the situation.
Guilt	When we've done something that goes against our values.	Stop the behavior causing guilt; make repairs (for example, apologize).	Continue the behavior; don't apologize or try to make repairs in other ways.
Shame	When we've done something that will cause us to be rejected by people we care about. When there's something about us (a personal characteristic) that would cause others to reject us if they found out.	Disconnect from others, isolate yourself. Judge yourself.	Reach out to others who are likely to accept and support you; connect; share what you're feeling shame about. Change self-judgments to nonjudgments; radically accept; self-validate.

Emotion	When Is It Justified?	Urge	How to Act Opposite
Jealousy	When an important relationship is in danger of being lost or taken away. When we fear we'll lose or have an important belonging taken away.	Act aggressively or violently toward the person you feel threatened by. Try to control the person you're afraid of losing (for example, interrogating or spying, snooping, or accusing them of being unfaithful). Be more clinging and dependent. Increase demonstrations of love (like trying to spend more time together).	Use skills to reregulate your emotions so you don't act aggressively or violently. Practice mindfulness, being in the present with the person rather than catastrophizing about the future. Practice being willing to have the discomfort of the fear of losing the person or object.
Envy	When an individual or group of people has something that we want.	Act in ways to make the other person look bad to others. Try to take away or ruin what the other person has. Judge the person.	Validate your feelings of envy and see if you can put them to good use, motivating yourself to work hard to get the things you want. Practice being grateful for the things you have. Practice nonjudgmental stance.

Looking at this chart you'll notice that with some emotions (anger, shame, jealousy, and envy are probably the most common), acting opposite to the emotion isn't just about outward behaviors, but also *thinking* opposite by taking a nonjudgmental stance. Judging others usually fuels our anger toward them, and self-judgments contribute to feelings such as shame. Remember that when we judge, we add fuel to our emotional fire, so thinking opposite by taking a nonjudgmental stance will reduce our emotional pain and help us get to our wise mind.

It's important to know that sometimes you'll want to act opposite when your emotions *are* justified. Facing discrimination in your workplace is a good example, because your anger is justified. Even when anger is justified, often it's so intense that getting to our wise mind and acting effectively in the situation is difficult. When this is the case, acting opposite to anger will help reduce the emotion so we can focus on working toward our goals.

Shame is another good example. Even if shame is justified (for example, you lied to your partner, you cheated on an exam, or you have a criminal record that you know people in your life would judge you for), having intense shame can actually be dangerous, leading to behaviors like substance abuse, self-harm, and even suicide. So, act opposite to shame. Find someone (a therapist, your best friend, a support group) you can connect with who will give you the validating, understanding response you need to help reduce the shame. (And, of course, learn from your shame: stop the behavior causing it, and don't do the behavior again.)

Though we're focusing on the emotions that are commonly viewed as painful, you may also want to act opposite to emotions that are often seen as pleasurable, such as joy or love. This might sound strange, but even pleasurable emotions might cause problems for us in certain situations: if you're in an unhealthy relationship, for example, acting opposite to love can help reduce those intense feelings over time. Or if you have a business meeting to attend soon after receiving the fantastic news that you're getting a promotion, you may want to act opposite to your joy for the next couple of hours!

When learning new skills, it can be helpful to analyze our behaviors after the fact, so here's a worksheet that will help you consider the outcome of acting opposite to your emotion or acting on the urge. Even when we don't use a skill for some reason (we forgot, or we just fell back into our old pattern), doing this kind of analysis can help us learn why we didn't use our skills so we'll be more likely to use them in future. I provided a sample worksheet and a blank one for you, and you can download more blank worksheets at this book's website: http://www.newharbinger.com/49647.

Opposite to Emotion Action Worksheet

Situation	Emotion	Action Urge	Action Taken	Aftereffects
(What event prompted the emotion or emotions?)	(What emotion or emotions did you experience?)	(What urge was attached to the emotion you experienced?)	(What actual action did you take?)	(What were the consequences of the behavior? For example, did emotion mind increase or decrease? Did your needs get met? Did you have regrets?)
I had a disagreement with my best friend.	I felt angry and hurt about the things they said to me.	I wanted to lash out at them and hurt them back.	I bit my tongue, told them I didn't think it was a good idea to continue speaking right now, and hung up the phone. Then I worked on nonjudgmental stance and distracted myself so I wouldn't keep dwelling on it.	My anger dissipated, although my hurt remained (Maybe less?). I'm glad I didn't react the way I wanted to in the moment, because that would've made things worse and increased my emotions. I know we'll be able to resolve this, and not lashing out has allowed me to get to my wise mind.

Opposite to Emotion Action Worksheet

Situation	Emotion	Action Urge	Action Taken	Aftereffects
(What event prompted the emotion or emotions?)	(What emotion or emotions did you experience?)	(What urge was attached to the emotion you experienced?)	(What actual action did you take?)	(What were the consequences of the behavior? For example, did emotion mind increase or decrease? Did your needs get met? Did you have regrets?)

Remember, the more you use skills when things are going relatively smoothly in your life, the more you'll be able to draw on them when things get difficult and those problematic urges arise. And, of course, remember also that the more you practice the skills you're learning in this book, the less often you'll experience those emotional hijacks and the more you'll be able to act effectively, bringing skills to bear and working toward your long-term goals. We'll look at the skill of being effective next.

Being Effective

Being effective has us identify our long-term goals, and then act skillfully from our wise mind to reach those goals (Linehan 2014). You've probably heard the saying "Don't cut off your nose to spite your face," meaning that you shouldn't let your emotion mind lead to behaviors you'll regret later. We all act in *ineffective* ways at times, letting our emotions or logic rule us rather than acting from our wise mind. This can have negative consequences. (Remember Chanda, who kept leaving jobs out of anger, and Kathrine, who had a habit of disregarding her emotions when making important decisions?) When responding to situations that bring up emotions, we want to aim for *effectiveness*.

What Gets in the Way?

Being effective might sound straightforward, but like many things, it's often easier said than done! There are several things that can get in the way.

NOT KNOWING OUR GOALS

Losing sight of long-term goals often gets in the way of us being effective. And, of course, taking the time to consider our goals means getting to our wise mind, which might be difficult, especially if there's some kind of short-term satisfaction from acting a certain way in the moment. Chanda, again, is a good example here, quitting her job reactively when experiencing intense emotions, rather than focusing on her long-term goals of increasing her financial stability and learning skills that will help her find a fulfilling career. Chanda might feel a sense of satisfaction (temporarily) when she quits a job out of anger, leaving her employer in the lurch, but in the long run the behavior is not helping her work toward her long-term goals; she's not being effective.

REFUSING TO SEE REALITY AS IT IS

We have a tendency to react to how we think a situation *should* be rather than responding to reality as it actually is (Linehan 2005), which gets in the way of being effective. Recall a time when you thought to yourself that something wasn't *fair*, or *shouldn't* be a certain way. If you think the speed limit on the road you're driving should be sixty miles per hour instead of forty miles per hour, you might end up sitting by the side of the road for an extra fifteen minutes while the nice police officer writes up your speeding ticket, which isn't effective if your long-term goal is to get where you're going as quickly as possible! Or if you have the thought that you shouldn't have to tell your partner how you feel (They should just know!), and this stops you from communicating your feelings, you're not working toward your long-term goal of having a healthy relationship. To determine if your behavior is effective, it can be helpful to ask yourself, *Is it more important that I be right, or that I get what I want?* (Linehan 2005). Being effective certainly doesn't mean giving up our values, but often it means giving up being right.

WILLFULNESS

Willfulness, something that all of us, as human beings, are familiar with, can also get in our way of being effective (Linehan 2014). Sometimes things get too painful, and we don't want to keep putting energy and effort into feeling better; we just want to take a break and pretend everything is fine. So we throw up our hands and say "whatever," or otherwise give up. Willfulness is refusing to try. Sometimes willfulness involves trying to control a situation so we don't have to experience something uncomfortable, such as difficult emotions, thoughts, or physical sensations. Obviously, when we're being willful, we're not being effective. So, the antidote is to get ourselves to a more willing place.

Being *willing* means that, although we might not like an experience, we remain open to it instead of closing ourselves off (May 1982). *Willingness* means that we refuse to give up, and we do our best with what we've got, even if we're not very hopeful of the outcome.

When willfulness shows up, the first step is to accept it: acknowledge that willfulness has arisen, and do your best to not judge it. Once you've done this, you can use the following strategies to help you get to a more willing place:

- Use a skill (or two or three!) to regulate your emotions: do a forward bend, stick your face in cold water, or do paced breathing to help you think more clearly.

- Change the expression on your face to change how you feel: putting a half smile on will help you feel more willing.

- Open up your posture to get to a more willing place. When we're feeling willful our muscles will typically tense up, and our posture will reflect our closed-off attitude: arms folded across the chest, fists clenched. Willingness is about opening up—unfolding, unclenching, and relaxing our muscles. Like our facial expression, our body language can also influence our emotions, so take a *willing posture* (Linehan 2014), letting your arms hang loosely at your sides and spreading your fingers wide. Taking slow, deep breaths will also help you feel more open and willing.

Getting to a more willing place will increase the likelihood that you'll be able to get to your wise mind and act effectively to get relief from painful emotions. Now that you're aware of some things that can get in the way of being effective and what to do about them, let's get you thinking about integrating this skill into your own life.

How Can You Be More Effective?

First, think of a situation—a current one or one you expect in the future—in which you might find yourself acting in ineffective ways, perhaps giving you some short-term satisfaction but ultimately moving you away from your long-term goals. Examples include saying something out of anger to a colleague, road-raging, or giving your partner the silent treatment. Make some notes about the anticipated situation.

_____

_____

_____

Recalling that being effective requires an awareness of your long-term goals, consider what goals you have generally in your life, or in the specific problematic situation.

_____

_____

While acting effectively won't guarantee that you'll get what you want in a situation, it will increase your chances of reaching your goals. See if you can come up with some skills that might help you move in that direction.

_____

_____

Now, consider what might be getting in the way of you reaching these goals.

_____

_____

What skills do you think you need to use to help you overcome these obstacles?

_____

_____

Let's turn now to a rescue skill that can help you be more willing and effective.

Rescue Skill: Taking an Open Posture

Our mind and body are irrevocably connected, so adopting a willing posture increases our receptiveness to an experience by influencing our mind to be more willing.

Sitting with your back fairly straight and your feet flat on the floor (if that's comfortable), tune in to your breath. Notice how it feels to breathe, drawing the air in through your nose. If you can, deepen your breathing. Feel the air expand your lungs as you inhale, and notice your lungs deflate as you exhale through your mouth or your nose, whichever is more comfortable. Now turn your attention to the rest of your body, noticing your posture and slowly opening it up:

Roll your shoulders back.

Open up your heart by pointing your chest toward the ceiling.

Open your hands wide, spreading your fingers as far apart as you can.

If you'd like, sweep your arms over your head and reach for the sky, keeping your fingers wide.

For additional willingness, add the half smile skill you learned in chapter 6!

Notice when your attention wanders, and gently, without judging, return your attention to the present—the feel of your breath and your body opening up. Continue to breathe and maintain this willing, open posture for as long or as short a time as you'd like.

You can practice this mindfulness exercise reactively (when you find yourself feeling willful or struggling to accept something) and proactively (just for the sake of practicing). The more you practice, the more willing and accepting you'll feel on a regular basis.

Wrapping Up

In this chapter you learned skills to help you change your emotions (through acting opposite) or a situation (through being effective). You also learned about how willfulness can get in your way, how being more willing will help you to be more effective, and strategies to help you get to that more willing place.

Remember, you can't learn these skills by just reading about them; practice is key, so take your time and do your best to learn and use them. In the next chapter we'll focus less on what to do with painful emotions and more on how to increase pleasurable ones.

CHAPTER 8

The Building Blocks of Pleasurable Emotions

So far in this workbook you've learned many skills to help you manage painful emotions more effectively. This chapter is about the other part of the equation, though: looking at making changes in your life so that enjoyable events will happen more often, increasing the pleasurable emotions you'll experience and enhancing your ability to manage difficult situations and emotions as they arise.

Be Mindful of the Positives

Think about moments in your life when you might experience some kind of little pleasure: your dog greets you at the door with unconditional love, sitting outside on a sunny day, sharing a smile with a stranger. How often do you think you miss noticing these moments? It can be easy to overlook feelings of calm, peace, contentment, and so on that you experience, especially when life is chaotic and busy, or when you're experiencing a lot of emotional pain. But with mindfulness practice, you'll be more able to notice the pleasure in life, even when it's only there for a short time or when the pleasurable emotion isn't an intense one like happiness or joy. The bottom line is, it's important to stop and smell the roses! Not only can doing so lead to more pleasurable moments, but it can change our body chemistry to help us feel good in the moment.

Activities That Generate Pleasurable Emotions

The following list of activities are proven to change our body chemistry to help us feel good. Of course, not every skill will fit every person, so you're going to need to try them out to figure out which ones work best for you.

Get out in nature. Just twenty minutes of exposure to a natural forest setting has been shown to significantly reduce a digestive enzyme called salivary alpha amylase, which is a marker of stress.

Compared to a group sitting in a city park with no trees, study participants who sat in the woods experienced an eightfold decrease in salivary alpha amylase and reported significantly less stress (Beil and Hanes 2013).

Humming, chanting, and singing. Humming, chanting a mantra, and energetic singing increase heart rate variability (HRV), which is another indicator of the body's stress level. A low HRV means you're more stressed, whereas a high HRV means you're less stressed. In addition, singing at the top of your lungs works the muscles in the back of the throat to activate the vagus nerve, one of the main components of the parasympathetic nervous system (PNS). And singing with others offers a double whammy, as it generates oxytocin, known as the "love hormone" because it makes people feel more connected to one another! Oxytocin also calms the amygdala, the part of our brain responsible for the emotional hijack, and temporarily prevents the release of stress hormones.

Reach out and touch someone. Hugging and holding hands releases oxytocin and reduces stress and feelings of loneliness. Even a pat on the back or a friendly handshake will help!

Laughter. Laughter also stimulates the vagus nerve, activating the PNS, and research has shown that when we laugh with a group of people our HRV increases, indicating lower stress levels (Dolgoff et al. 2012). So read the funny pages, turn on the comedy channel, or look into laughing yoga or laughing meditation—yep, both are a thing!

Listen to music. Research has found that areas of the brain release dopamine—known as the "feel-good neurotransmitter"—when we listen to our favorite music. So yes, there's a biological reason why music makes us feel good!

The important thing, of course, is to find activities that generate pleasurable emotions for *you*, and to find activities that you can do every day. Here's a list of additional options to get you thinking:

Talk to someone positive in your life.

Go for a walk or a drive.

Read.

Look at photos of your last vacation.

Pet your cat or play with your dog.

Go sit by the ocean, a lake, or a river.

Make plans or fantasize about your next vacation.

Paint your toenails or give yourself a facial.

Listen to some of your favorite music.

Watch online videos of baby animals.

Think about what life will be like when you retire, finish school, get your dream job, and so on.

Keeping these examples in mind, let's get you thinking about what activities might work for you.

Finding Your Activities

In the space provided, list any activities you can think of that have brought you some kind of pleasurable emotions. The activity might not generate "enjoyment" or "fun," but at least some kind of pleasure (calm, contentment, interest, soothing, peace, and so on). If there are things you've done in the past that have helped you feel better, start with these.

_____   _____

_____   _____

_____   _____

If you're having difficulties, don't worry; you might need to really brainstorm in order to think of activities that might be pleasurable for you in some way, so let's try that.

Write down anything you can think of, even if it seems unrealistic (Don't limit yourself!), that you think might generate any of those pleasurable emotions I mentioned.

_____   _____

_____   _____

_____   _____

If you're still struggling to think of activities, consider anything that's ever appealed to you. For example, maybe you saw a TV show about scuba diving and that activity seemed interesting—write it down! Or maybe you have a friend who plays squash or pickleball and that sounded like fun—add it to your list. If still nothing comes to mind, it's time for research: Google "fun things to do" or "enjoyable activities." You'll be surprised at how many lists are out there, and these may get you started with your own list. You can also ask family and friends for suggestions. Add whatever you come up with to your list.

Once you've got your list, choose one activity to start with. You might find that some things on your list aren't feasible in the short term—maybe scuba diving is too expensive for you right now. While starting a new hobby can be a lot of fun, planning for it can give you pleasure as well, so consider how you might be able to work toward doing an activity that seems out of reach. For example, start reading about scuba diving or marine life. Go to a local dive shop to talk to people about what you need to know to decide if diving might be for you. Saving for an activity can also give you a sense of satisfaction, and if you have someone to share this adventure with, making plans together can increase the fun. The point is that even if something on your list isn't doable just yet, you can still get pleasure out of it in other ways.

Make some notes here about what activity you'll start with, and what you'll do to try that activity now or work toward it:

_____

_____

_____

And don't worry, if you're stuck still trying to think of pleasurable activities, the next section on goal setting will likely help!

Setting Goals

Setting goals is also important when it comes to generating pleasurable emotions, and, as we experience a sense of pride in ourselves for reaching a goal, goal setting will also typically result in us building mastery (see chapter 5). Even if we don't achieve all of our goals, just having long- and short-term goals will give us something to look forward to, contributing to pleasurable emotions. If we don't have goals in life, a sense of where we'd like to be and what we'd like to be doing, we can experience a sense of being unfulfilled or stuck. Setting goals isn't always easy, and the following exercise can help you with it.

What Are Your Goals?

First, let's go back to brainstorming. In the space provided, write down any goals that come to mind. For each time frame, consider where you'd like to you see yourself. Perhaps you'd like to see yourself managing your emotions more effectively. What about work? Are you happy with your job? Do you have aspirations to return to school? Is there something you started earlier in life you'd like to finish? What about relationships—romantic, friendships, family? Are they satisfying, or do you need to work on improving or even ending them? Would you like to travel? Do some volunteer work? It can also be helpful to ask yourself, *What would I do if I had six months to live?* What would you want to change in your life? This mental exercise can put things into perspective!

Six months: _____

_____

One year: _____

_____

Five years: _____

_____

Next, reviewing each of your lists, choose just one to two goals that you'll start with. Keep in mind that when it comes to goal setting, less is more. If you tackle too many goals at once, you'll likely end up feeling overwhelmed and will struggle to move toward any of your goals. You can always come back for the others later! It can also be helpful to have goals in each time frame that are connected, so that while you're working on your five-year goal of being in a serious and committed relationship, for example, some of your six-month and one-year goals are moving you in that same direction (like learning to manage your emotions more effectively so you can be in a healthy relationship).

Having a visual reminder of our goals that we see on a daily basis is another thing that can help us work toward them. Regular exposure to what we want to achieve works on both a conscious and unconscious level. This visual cue can be simple: write your goal down on a sticky note and place it somewhere you'll see it daily. Or, if you're more creative, you could make a vision board, collage, or something else to represent the goal. It's up to you, but remember, goal setting is part of your larger goal of managing emotions more effectively, because the more positives you have in your life, here in the form of reaching for and achieving goals, the better you'll be able to deal with the painful stuff when it arises.

Find Connection with Others

We'll be looking more closely at relationships in the next chapter, but because they have so many implications for our emotional health, it's important for you to start considering them now.

Relationships bring us love, connection, and support. They also bring us joy and fulfillment, as well as a lot of pain. Like it or not, we are social creatures, and we need relationships in order to thrive. In fact, research has shown that loneliness and social isolation can lead to various psychiatric disorders and *physical* health problems. One study even found that a lack of social connection carried health risks similar to smoking up to fifteen cigarettes a day (Holt-Lunstad et al. 2015)!

It's important to recognize that everyone has different needs for connection. Some people need many close friends and acquaintances to feel satisfied, whereas others are happy with a very small group of people whom they're close to. Therefore it's important to ask your wise mind if you have enough relationships in your life, or if something is missing for you in this realm. It can be difficult to answer this, and I emphasize the need to listen to your wise mind here, because many people experience social anxiety or depression, or have had negative experiences that contribute to an unbalanced perspective on relationships (for example, *There's no point in getting close to others, because people will always hurt me,* or *I'm too much for people to handle because of my intense emotions*). When I asked one of my clients if she thought she had enough relationships in her life, she responded, "I don't *want* more relationships in my life, but I know I *need* more relationships in my life," indicating to me that her emotion mind was in conflict with her wise mind.

Take a moment to get to your wise mind and ask yourself, *Do I have enough social connections? Is this an area in which I'm missing something?* What does your wise mind tell you? If you don't have an answer just yet, don't worry. As I said, we'll return to this topic in the next chapter.

Express Your Gratitude

Gratitude is the quality of being thankful for or feeling appreciative of what we have—you know, the idea of counting your blessings. Of course, while gratitude involves noticing the positive things happening in the world around us, it doesn't mean ignoring the problematic or painful things. That would be avoidance! While this whole idea of "practicing gratitude" might seem cliché, research actually backs this practice up as something that contributes to our emotional and physical well-being. Let's look first at some of these benefits before turning to how to foster a gratitude practice.

While research on gratitude is still limited, there is evidence that it can improve well-being; increase resilience, compassion, and satisfaction in life; strengthen relationships; reduce stress and depression; and enhance the capacity for pleasurable emotions (Emmons and McCullough 2003; Sheldon and Lyubomirsky 2007). There's also evidence that gratitude can have positive effects on our physical health, lowering blood pressure (Shipon 2007) and improving sleep quality (Wood et al. 2009), both of which contribute to our mental health, including emotion regulation.

While gratitude often arises as a spontaneous emotion, there's benefit to practicing it consciously, because the more we practice, the more we strengthen the brain's neural circuits for this emotion, making it easier to experience gratitude. When we practice focusing on the positive things we have, our brain becomes more adept at discovering similar things; in other words, as with any skill, the more we practice gratitude, the better we get at it! So how do we do this? Expressing it in some way is key. There are lots of ways to do this, and here are some ideas.

Keep a gratitude journal. Each evening write down three things you were grateful for that day.

Write a gratitude letter to someone. Write a letter, preferably by hand, describing the effect someone has had on your life. It could be someone in your life presently, or someone from your past (it could even be to someone who's no longer living), say a mentor or teacher, a coworker or boss, or a friend or partner (or ex!). It could be someone you don't know personally but who had an impact on your life in some way, such as a political figure or philanthropist. It could be a pet—really anyone. Whether you send the letter or not, of course, is up to you!

Listen to a guided gratitude meditation. There are lots of apps available for this!

Be mindful when someone is thanking you, paying you a compliment, or saying something else that makes you feel good. Notice if this is difficult for you, and if it is, just notice the emotions that arise without judgment.

Take a daily photo of something you're grateful for. You might choose to post it to social media to share your gratitude with others—or you might not!

Rescue Skill: Taking on an Attitude of Gratitude

Before we finish this chapter, let's look at how you can also use gratitude practice as a rescue skill. While it can be challenging to feel thankful while in a crisis, gratitude can help us manage our emotions effectively to get through difficult, emotionally charged times.

Before employing this rescue skill, you might first need to turn to one of the fast-acting skills (like the forward bend, cold water, and so on) we've covered to get your emotions somewhat regulated. Over time, you'll likely need these skills less often as you turn to other skills that help you prevent the emotional hijacking from happening in the first place, but until that's the case, be sure to use whatever skills you need to prevent yourself from making a situation even more difficult.

Once you've reduced the intensity of the emotion (or if you were able to catch it before it became intense), focus on something you feel grateful for. It might be someone in your life now or from your past, your job, the roof over your head, the country you live in, and so forth. (When I'm feeling angry at the most recent problem life has sent my way, I hear myself thinking *first-world problems*. I don't mean this in a self-judgmental way, but rather as a reminder that I have so many things to be grateful for—things I might not have had I been born in another part of the world.)

The key with this practice, of course, is finding what works for you. It's important to make sure you're not invalidating your experience, rather you're reminding yourself of what you can be grateful for, turning your attention to those people or things instead of staying focused on the problem. You might find it helpful to combine this rescue skill with other skills, such as taking an open posture, putting on a half smile, validating your emotions, distracting yourself from the problem, practicing accepting reality, or paced breathing. In fact, it's always important to not forget to breathe!

Wrapping Up

In this chapter we turned our focus from managing painful emotions to generating pleasure by creating more opportunities for positive events through identifying pleasurable activities, setting goals, connecting with others, and practicing gratitude. In the next chapter we'll look more closely at the importance of relationships in your life, assessing the relationships you have (or don't have!) and how they might be contributing to your painful emotions. I'll cover skills to help you develop relationships, if you don't currently have enough, and make the ones you have healthier and more satisfying. Even if you don't think you need these relationship skills, I encourage you to at least take a peek at the chapter, because most of us can benefit from developing skills that help us to be more effective with others in our life!

CHAPTER 9

The Importance of Relationships

As I mentioned in the last chapter, human beings are social creatures, and the effects of social isolation and loneliness are profound, not just for our emotional well-being, but for our physical health. All humans need relationships in order to thrive. That said, managing relationships is sometimes easier said than done!

Relationships often contribute to emotion dysregulation. For some this might be in the form of not having enough connections and thus feeling lonely and isolated. For many it's in the form of anxiety: fearing that others will be angry with us or will end our relationship, worrying about how others perceive us, and struggling to be more assertive in getting our wants and needs met. Most humans want to be accepted and liked by others, so rest assured it's not unusual for interactions with others to be such a source of turmoil.

Many of the skills you've learned in this workbook will help with relationships, but in this chapter we'll look specifically at skills to help you create satisfying, balanced relationships (whether these are existing relationships or new ones), and at important considerations to keep your relationships healthy. First, let's take a look at the relationships you currently have in your life, as always, starting with awareness.

Increasing Your Awareness of Your Relationships

As you already know, you first have to be aware of reality as it is before you can decide if you want or need to make changes. So, returning to a question I posed in the last chapter, Do you have enough relationships in your life, or is something missing in this realm? There is no black-and-white answer to this question, and because we all have different needs socially, you need to strive for a balanced perspective. Here are some prompts to help you answer this question from your wise mind.

Write the names of the people to whom you feel closest. (Don't worry if you don't see or talk to them often, just consider the closeness of the relationships.)

_____

_____

When you want to spend quality time with someone, who do you think of? (List all the people who come to mind.)

_____

_____

If you want to get out of the house and do something—watch a movie, go for dinner, take a walk in the park, or whatever—who can you call to keep you company?

_____

_____

If you're feeling troubled, have a problem you're struggling with, or are in crisis, who are you comfortable talking to?

_____

_____

Are there any groups—religious, volunteer, or support—you belong to through which you feel supported?

_____

_____

Imagine yourself in a crisis, struggling with intense emotions, whatever that looks like for you. If you have a go-to person (like your partner, parent, or best friend), imagine that person isn't currently available for some reason. Who would you turn to instead?

_____

Now imagine that your backup person is on vacation (or at work, or otherwise unavailable). Who else would you turn to?

_____

Take a minute now to review your answers. Does anything stand out? Make some notes here.

_____

_____

While everyone has different needs for social interactions and support, everyone does have these needs. I've worked with clients who tell me they don't need relationships, but this simply isn't true: human beings are not meant to be alone. We can survive on our own, but we thrive when we're part of a community. Ongoing difficulties with depressed mood, shame, loneliness, and so on will usually be made worse by isolation. So in reviewing your responses to the previous questions, see if your wise mind has an answer to this question: Do you have enough relationships, or do you need more? If you're struggling to come up with an answer, you might try doing a Pros and Cons Chart (see chapter 1) for developing new relationships. This exercise can also help you identify what might be getting in the way of you being open to increasing the social and supportive connections you have in your life.

Increasing Connections

For some, answering that question is the easy part; it's doing something about it that's more difficult. If you recognize that you need more relationships, you'll have to consider how you're going to go about increasing them. Here are some ideas.

RECONNECT WITH PEOPLE

Reconnecting with someone you used to have a relationship with is a good way to increase the number of people in your life. Think of people from your past: someone from school or a previous job with whom you lost touch, neighbors from your old community, someone with whom you attended a support group. Even if there's someone with whom you had a falling out, you might want to consider trying to work things out and rekindling this friendship. That may seem daunting, but the worst-case scenario might be you having some sort of closure, and the best-case scenario might be you reengaging a relationship that was important to you.

STRENGTHEN CURRENT RELATIONSHIPS

If reconnecting with someone isn't an option, think about people you interact with on a more superficial level: a casual acquaintance, such as a neighbor, a coworker, or someone you chat with in yoga class or at a coffee shop. With whom might you deepen a current connection, turning it into more of a friendship? Ask your coworker if they'd like to grab a coffee at break, or strike up a conversation with that person in yoga after class has ended, and see where it takes you.

FIND NEW PEOPLE

If the first two suggestions aren't viable options for you, or you've tried them to no avail, try putting yourself in a new situation, where you can meet new people who might become friends. Especially for people who experience anxiety, this is a difficult option because it involves not only new people, but new situations, which may mean going way out of one's comfort zone. If this option makes you nervous, but it seems like a good one to explore, keep in mind that you have the tools you need to regulate your anxiety. The skills you've learned in this workbook—such as regulating your body chemistry, practicing mindfulness, validation, acting opposite, being effective, and so on—can help you act from your wise mind while trying to meet new people.

If you're committed to finding new people, consider what situations will work best for you. You could join a new class at the gym (Or join a gym!), or try something as simple as smiling at people you pass while walking. You might be surprised at the responses you get! Perhaps a social hobby, such as a knitting or scrapbooking club, or a class, such as scuba diving or photography, sounds like a good option. You could try meeting people while doing volunteer work.

Remember, it can be helpful to write down your goal, so if increasing relationships is something you need to work on, make a note of that here, and one step you're willing to take in that direction.

_____

_____

In the next section we'll look at some skills to help you make these new relationships healthy ones, and to keep them that way.

Observing Your Limits

In DBT, _observing your limits_ is the process of noticing whether someone's behavior is acceptable to you. Read the following examples, and in the space provided write your thoughts and feelings about each situation. It can be an interesting experiment to ask a friend or family member to give you their thoughts about these situations as well, if you're comfortable doing this, and comparing your responses.

Your friend knows you have to be up early in the morning, yet they often call you after 11 p.m.

_____

_____

You've had plans for a few weeks to go out for dinner with your friend. An hour before you're supposed to meet at the restaurant, they call you to tell you they can't make it.

_____

_____

You're meeting your friend for lunch. They forgot their wallet and ask you to cover the bill.

_____

_____

If you had someone else look at these situations, compare your responses. Were they the same, or were some of your reactions different? If they're different, this is a good example of dialectics: there's no *right* or *wrong* in these situations, just different perspectives. If you did this exercise alone, what do your answers say to you? You might notice that your reaction depends on the circumstances: "It depends on the reason for their late-night call," or "It depends on why they canceled," or "It depends on the status of my relationship with this friend." Observing our limits is about considering how we think and feel about someone's behavior, and if it's not okay for us, doing something about it.

The Consequences of Not Observing Limits

Allowing behavior that we find problematic or unacceptable to continue typically leads to feelings of resentment and burnout in a relationship. Can you think of an example of this from your life? I had a good friend from high school from whom I was feeling more and more distant. It seemed that I always had to reach out to her, and it felt like our friendship wasn't as important to her as it was to me. Instead of addressing the problem by talking to her about it, I grew resentful, I stopped reaching out to her, and the relationship just ended. (Something I still regret!) Are any of your relationships pushing your limits? Make some notes here.

_____

_____

_____

How to Observe Your Limits

Of course, the first step in observing our limits is noticing that a behavior that's happening is not acceptable for us. My early warning sign for when someone is pushing my limits is that I start to feel irritable with that person, and I typically feel less willing to be around them. What are your early warning signs? (You may have to come back to this question after observing your reaction the next time someone is pushing a limit with you).

_____

_____

Be sure not to assume the other person knows their behavior is problematic for you. Everyone has different limits, and our limits may even change depending on the circumstances. We might not even know we have a certain limit until we experience it being pushed, so how can we expect others to know?

Once we become aware of the reaction we're having, and that we need to observe a limit with someone, the next step is to figure out how to communicate this. This is where anxiety often arises for people: _What if the other person gets angry, or even ends the relationship?_ Remember, if you ignore your limits often, you'll typically end up resenting the other person, which will likely lead to an explosion of some sort (for example, lashing out or ending the relationship altogether, when that may not be what you actually want). Do these possibilities ring bells for you? Do you tend to ignore your warning signs? If so, what have the consequences been?

_____

_____

_____

As scary or intimidating as the prospect of observing your limits can be, it is a necessary part of any relationship. And communicating in healthy ways is key to observing your limits, so let's look at this topic next.

The Importance of Healthy Communication

One of the most common relationship problems I encounter with clients is difficulty communicating with others, which is often related to emotions getting in the way. As I mentioned earlier, people often fear how others will respond if they try to observe a limit or communicate some other need. Sometimes people think they're not deserving of what they want, judge themselves as "selfish" or feel ashamed for trying to get a need met, don't realize they have an unmet need or want, or simply don't know how to effectively ask for things, so they choose avoidance instead. Regardless of the reason, the results are generally the same: more emotional pain that will increase the likelihood of an emotional hijack and target behaviors happening at some point. This chain of events illustrates why communication skills are so important when we talk about managing emotions.

To learn how to communicate effectively, you need to first ask yourself, *What's getting in the way of me communicating effectively?* Then, of course, you need to start working on the roadblocks you discover. Let's start by identifying your current communication style, and then we'll look at skills that will help you be more assertive.

Communication Styles

Most people typically communicate with a particular style or two: passive, aggressive, passive-aggressive, or assertive. While we need to think of this dialectically, recognizing that how we communicate will depend on many factors, including the person we're communicating with and the context of the situation, it's also important to understand our predominate patterns. To help you learn more about each of the different communication styles, and to identify your predominant styles, take the following quiz.

Communication Styles Quiz

Read each statement and put a check beside the ones that seem to describe you best (the ones that apply to you *usually*, or *most often*). Add up the number of checkmarks in each section to see which communication styles you use most often.

Passive

- ☐ I push my feelings away rather than express them to others.

- ☐ I worry that expressing myself will cause others to be angry with me or to not like me.

- ☐ I often hear myself saying "I don't care" or "It doesn't matter" when I do care, and it does matter.

- ☐ I try not to rock the boat, keeping quiet because I don't want to upset others.

- ☐ I often go along with others' opinions because I don't want to be different.

Total: _____

Aggressive

- ☐ I'm concerned with getting my own way, regardless of how it affects others.

- ☐ I often yell, swear, or use other aggressive means of communicating.

- ☐ My friends and coworkers are often afraid of or intimidated by me.

- ☐ I don't really care if others get what they need as long as my needs are met.

- ☐ I've heard others say that I have an "It's my way or the highway" attitude.

Total: _____

Passive-Aggressive

- ☐ I have a tendency to be sarcastic in conversations with others as a way of indirectly expressing myself.

- ☐ I tend to give people the silent treatment when I'm angry with them.

- ☐ I often find myself saying one thing but thinking another.

- ☐ I'm generally reluctant to express my emotions in words, resorting instead to aggressive behaviors, like slamming doors.

- ☐ I try to get my message across in more subtle ways for fear that expressing myself will cause others to be angry with me or to stop liking me.

Total: _____

Assertive

- ☐ I believe I have the right to express my opinions and emotions.

- ☐ When I'm having a disagreement with someone, I express my opinions and emotions clearly and honestly.

- ☐ In communicating with others, I treat them with respect while also respecting myself.

- ☐ I listen closely to what others are saying, sending the message that I'm trying to understand their perspective.

- ☐ I try to negotiate with the other person if we have different goals rather than just focusing on getting my own needs met.

Total: _____

Which communication style did you score the highest on? Does this surprise you? Did this quiz help you to understand where some of your difficulties in relationships might stem from? Make some notes here.

_____

_____

_____

_____

The next step, of course, is to learn some skills to help you communicate more effectively. If you scored highest on the assertive communication style, by the way, these skills can still be helpful. We can never be *too* assertive, and you never know when more people skills will come in handy!

How to Communicate Assertively

Being *assertive* means expressing your emotions and thoughts in a clear way, and in a way that's respectful both of yourself and others. It involves caring about others and their needs, and trying to understand their perspectives. Using this communication style often means negotiation and compromise as you try to meet your own needs, as well as those of others.

I mentioned earlier that people sometimes struggle with being assertive because they don't feel they deserve to ask for things from others (or to say no to others' requests). If you don't feel good about yourself or like who you are as a person, it makes sense that you might struggle to communicate your thoughts and emotions to others. The good news is that asserting yourself will often increase feelings of self-respect and self-esteem, as well as improve your relationships, which will also help you to feel better about yourself.

Be Clear About Your Goals

The first step in being assertive is deciding what your goals are. If you're not clear on what you want out of the interaction, you'll likely struggle to communicate this clearly to others. Let's look at an example.

Celia described herself as a more sensitive person, feeling things deeply and recognizing her tendency to have stronger emotional reactions than others. While she had come to accept this about herself, it was something her family had never really understood, and even now as an adult their inability to let her have her emotions was something that got in the way of Celia being able to have close relationships with them.

After starting therapy with a new therapist who introduced Celia to DBT skills, Celia identified the goal of having closer relationships with her parents. Recognizing that she had grown up in a pervasively invalidating environment in which she regularly received the message that her emotions "made no sense" and that she was "overreacting," Celia also realized she had fallen into a pattern of invalidating her own emotions, and she and her therapist started talking about the importance of being more assertive. Celia decided to ask her parents to validate her emotions. She wanted to communicate to them that they didn't have to agree with or like how she was feeling, but she wanted them to not judge her, and to let her have her feelings.

The following DBT skills can help you be more assertive (Linehan 2014). I'll outline the skills first, and then we'll use Celia's example to look at how to put them into practice.

Describe the situation: It's helpful to begin by describing the situation you want to discuss with the other person. Stick to the facts of the situation, staying away from judgments and blaming. This is you laying the groundwork for the conversation; you're essentially describing for the other person what the conversation is about.

State your thoughts and emotions: Express what you're thinking and feeling. (Emotions will be optional, depending on who you're having the conversation with; for example, if you're being assertive with your coworker or boss, you may want to leave emotions out of it.) Remember not to judge or blame: you want the person to remain open to hearing what you have to say, and judgments and blame are a sure way to shut others down or put them on the defensive. Using "I" statements (for example, "*I feel hurt when* you don't return my calls") can help keep you on track here.

Clearly state what you want: Be specific about what you're asking for (or about saying no to the other person's request). This is where being clear on your goals will come in handy, so that you can make an explicit request or give a clear no. Remember that others can't read your mind!

Reinforce: It can be helpful to think of something positive the other person will get out of giving you what you're asking for; this way, they'll be more likely to want to help because they see that it's not just all about you, but that you're willing to give in order to get.

Let's turn back to Celia's story to see how she was assertive with her parents. Celia wrote the following script, with the help of her therapist, to ask her parents to validate her emotions.

Describe the situation: I often feel like you judge me when I'm feeling strong emotions; for example, last week when I was struggling with anxiety about going to the dentist, you told me I was "being ridiculous" and "acting like a child," and this just made me feel more things—like shame and disappointment in myself.

State your thoughts and emotions: I know I'm more emotional than you are, and I know it's often hard for you to understand why I feel the way I do about things. I also know that this is just who I am: I feel things more strongly than you do, but this isn't *bad*, it's just *different*.

Clearly state what you want: I'd like it if you could do your best to not judge me when I'm having strong feelings. You don't have to like it, or agree with how I'm feeling, but I want you to just let me have my feelings.

Reinforce: If I don't feel judged for my emotions I'll want to spend more time with you and will feel closer to you. It will also help me in the work I'm doing on being more accepting of myself and on managing my emotions in healthier ways.

Now it's your turn. Think of a conversation you need to have with someone. It can be anything: asking your partner to do a chore to free up some time so you can start exercising, calling your cell phone provider to discuss a problem with your bill, or asking your boss for a day off during a busy time. In the space provided, write out your script. (You can also use these skills to say no to someone's request, although you can likely do an abbreviated version. Nonetheless, when it comes to saying no, it can be helpful to state your opinions and emotions, and to clearly state what you want—in this case, to say no.)

Describe the situation: _____

_____

State your thoughts and emotions: _____

_____

Clearly state what you want: _____

_____

Reinforce: _____

_____

Once you've written your script, be sure to rehearse it; the more you practice it the more your confidence will grow and the easier the words will flow when you have the conversation. If it feels too difficult to say the words, start by reading the script (especially if it's a conversation with someone you're close to, who knows about the work you're doing on managing your emotions).

If you've struggled to be assertive, keep in mind that changing the way you communicate with others is often hard. If you're a more passive communicator, you may feel that being assertive is "aggressive," and if you're used to being on the more aggressive end of the spectrum, it may seem like being assertive is too passive and ineffective. Rest assured that this is the most effective and healthiest way of communicating, and over time you'll see that it will create more satisfying relationships for you. It's also likely to have you feeling better about yourself as you work on meeting others' needs as well as your own. These skills, like all the others you've been learning in this workbook, will probably take a lot of energy and practice initially, but they will come more naturally with time. The important thing, of course, is to practice, practice, practice!

Additional Skills for Assertiveness

These additional skills will help you work toward your goals and make it more likely that you'll maintain good relationships and even feel good about yourself after interactions in which you communicated assertively.

Mindfulness

I often hear clients describe themselves as "conflict avoidant," referring to their tendency to avoid having conversations about difficult things with people in their life out of fear of losing the person or damaging the relationship in some way. I like to remind them that *it's not a conflict, it's a conversation*. If Celia goes into the conversation with her parents thinking of it as a conflict, this could become a self-fulfilling prophecy and turn the conversation into an argument. If, on the other hand, she notices when her mind goes into the future and creates that imaginary scenario in which she's arguing with her parents, Celia can accept that her thoughts have wandered to the future (and perhaps to the past, as well, if this has been their pattern) and bring herself back to the present. Remember, when we're being mindful, we're more rooted in the present moment and we're more accepting of what's happening in that moment, which means less emotional pain; and less pain makes the conversation more manageable, with a reduced likelihood for negative consequences.

Mindfulness is also important in that it communicates to the other person that you're paying attention and are genuinely interested in the conversation. So eliminate potential distractions: take out your earbuds, put down your phone, and focus on the other person, giving them your full attention. Ask questions and be interested in their responses.

Validate

Remember the skill of self-validation that we went over in chapter 6, which you used to focus on accepting your emotions? Validating others will also go a long way in maintaining or even improving relationships. Can you recall a time when someone validated you? Do you remember how good it felt to know you were understood or accepted? Communicating to others that their experience is important, and that you understand or accept their perspective and emotions (Remember, doing this doesn't necessarily mean that you agree with them!) will greatly benefit your relationships.

Be Genuine and Use Humor

Being assertive doesn't necessarily mean you have to be all serious. When it's appropriate, feel free to lighten the mood of a conversation a little with a smile, laughter, and your sense of humor. Even if it's a serious conversation, this can reduce tension and improve the likelihood of a positive outcome.

Stick to Your Values

You're probably familiar with the golden rule to treat others as you want to be treated. Have you ever considered how, exactly, you treat others? Do you judge, blame, yell, and so on? You probably wouldn't want that treatment from others, right? When you're trying to get a need met, consider how you can make the other person want to help you.

At a clinic I once worked at, I remember a client who had become understandably impatient and angry after waiting thirty minutes for their psychiatrist. I offered to walk this person over to the receptionist to see if they might be able to track down the doctor; however, the client raised their voice toward me and threatened to pull the fire alarm if the psychiatrist didn't show up! This was definitely not an effective way of getting help! So, in a conversation, treat the other person the way you would like to be treated, and you'll be more likely to reach your goals.

Imagining that you have an audience for the interaction is another helpful tool for sticking to your values in a conversation. If people you respect were watching you, would you be embarrassed or ashamed? Or would you feel comfortable behaving the way you are? The answers to these questions can be good indicators of whether or not you're acting according with your values.

How We Learn to Be in Relationships

We've gone over skills to help us communicate more assertively with others, but assertiveness is only one means of creating healthy and satisfying relationships. Let's look at more skills you can use with this goal in mind.

Think about some of the things you've been "trained" to do in your life: say "please" and "thank you," say "excuse me" when you bump into someone, or sneeze into your elbow to prevent the spread of germs. We learn to be in relationships with others and others learn how to be in relationships with us in the same way. Think back to Celia, for example, who learned from her parents' judgmental responses that her strong emotional reactions weren't okay; as a result, she learned to stuff her emotions in order to avoid further invalidation. By the way, I'm not blaming Celia's parents; they may have been raised by parents who avoided emotions, so this is what they themselves learned. As a result of this style of learning, though, we end up doing more of what we're rewarded for and less of what we're punished or not rewarded for.

In the following section we're going to look at using behavioral principles to help you get to a healthier place with the people in your life, and to get more of what you want (and less of what you don't want) in your relationships.

Changing Patterns

If you have children, or have ever trained a pet, you're probably familiar with the principles—reinforcement and negative consequence—that I'm going to discuss here. Let's start with reinforcement. Consider a child throwing a temper tantrum in the grocery store: they want a chocolate bar, and their parent refuses to give it to them. What's the best thing to do? Not give in, of course! We don't want to reinforce the behavior of throwing a temper tantrum. The parent might also refuse to bring the child to the grocery store the next time, which is a negative consequence of the child throwing the temper tantrum, and which will (Hopefully!) make it less likely that they'll throw a tantrum again in future. Similarly, when you're training your dog and they come when you call, you give them a treat; when they don't come right away, they don't get a treat (no reinforcer) and they go back on the leash (a negative consequence).

Now, think of how these principles can be applied to relationships. To start, let's go back to Celia, who was asking her parents to validate her more. Ideally, when Celia's parents validate her, she'll reinforce them for their efforts: "It means a lot to me that you're trying to let me have my feelings," or "I know you're working hard to do what I asked of you, and I appreciate it." Celia might also reward her parents by spending more time with them. And, of course, when Celia's parents *in*validate her, spending less time with them will presumably be aversive for them, hopefully leading to a reduction in their invalidating behavior.

Consider a relationship with someone important to you, and how you might use these principles to make it healthier, by answering the following questions.

What would you like more of in that relationship? Perhaps like Celia it's validation, or maybe it's more time with a person or having them reach out to you more often if you feel that you put more energy into the relationship than they do. Write whatever thoughts come to mind.

_____

_____

_____

_____

_____

_____

What would you like less of in that important relationship? For example, would you like to reduce the conflict with someone whom you fight with a lot?

_____

_____

_____

_____

Now consider what reinforcers you might use in this relationship, and write them here. (It's important for you to know that providing positive consequences usually works better than negatives, so instead of telling someone you'll be likely to end the relationship if they don't spend more time with you, for example, you might express that you'll feel happier and more connected in the relationship if they spent more time with you.)

_____

_____

_____

_____

At some point you'll want to consider these same questions for the other important relationships in your life. Of course, before applying these principles it will be helpful to assertively communicate the changes you're looking for. And remember that the skills in this workbook don't come with guarantees: we can be as assertive as possible, using all of our skills, and still not get our needs met. But when we're observing our limits, assertively communicating those limits to others, and doing our best to provide reinforcers for the behaviors we want more of and we're _still_ not getting our needs met, it might be time to consider ending the relationship.

What to Do About Unhealthy Relationships

At times we may find ourselves in an unhealthy relationship, one in which we feel unsatisfied and aren't getting our needs met. We might feel stuck in the relationship for some reason (perhaps out of a sense of obligation or misplaced loyalty, or perhaps because we're lacking in relationships and so

This relationship is better than being alone). Unless a relationship is abusive or toxic in some way, ending it usually should be a last resort, the point at which you've used all the appropriate skills and nothing is changing. Let's explore important aspects of ending a relationship.

Make a Wise Choice

First, it's important that you make the decision to end the relationship from your wise mind. It can be easy to let emotions rule you when you get to a point of feeling so hurt or frustrated with someone that ending the relationship *feels* like the best thing to do, but making a decision like this from emotion mind is likely to lead to you regretting your decision later. If you choose to end the relationship, you want to be sure it is a wise choice, so take your time, and be sure to practice the skills you've been learning throughout this workbook to help you not get hijacked by your emotions. To help you get to that wise place, you can also use the Pros and Cons Chart that we looked at in chapter 1. I've included one here for you as well.

Pros of Ending the Relationship	Cons of Ending the Relationship
Pros of *Not* Ending the Relationship	Cons of *Not* Ending the Relationship

Remember, you can also score each item to help you see what's most important to you in making this decision.

Keep Yourself Safe

Everyone has the right to be physically and emotionally safe and respected, so if you're in a relationship (romantic, friendship, family, or otherwise) in which you're being abused in any way, you have the right to leave. If you're not sure how to do this, ask someone you trust for help, or call your local crisis line or shelter.

Rescue Skill: Creating A Secure Place

You might notice that some of your relationships change as you make changes in your life, which can cause growing pains: people might resist the changes you're making, even though they're positive changes, or you might find that when you're healthier and have more self-respect, things that used to be okay for you now push your limits. Keeping this in mind, let's turn to this chapter's rescue skill.

Removing yourself from a difficult situation can, of course, help when you're experiencing intense emotions; while it's not always possible to physically do this, you *can* leave the situation mentally using an imaginary *secure* (or *calm* or *healing*) *place.* A secure place is a real or fictional place you can experience in your mind and use to help you get away when things get difficult. In this place you'll feel secure, and you'll be able to take some time to regulate your emotions and feel calmer.

Consider what this place will look like for you. It can be a real place you've been to—perhaps a favorite vacation spot or a room in your home. If it's based in reality, however, it's important that you have no negative associations with the place; it should be a place where you'll be able to truly experience peace and security. And, of course, it can be a completely imagined place. I've had clients imagine themselves on a desert island (with all of the amenities they could want), on a space station, or at a campsite by a lake. It's also important that there are no other people in your secure place, since we can't control other people, even in our own imagination at times. Pets or other animals can be there if you wish, but no people allowed!

Once you have this place in mind, sit with it and develop it in as much detail as you can. What do you see as you look around you? Do you hear anything? Are there smells? What do you feel with your body? A gentle breeze, the warmth of the sun? Do your best to let this experience really sink in as much as possible, feeling its calm, healing properties. Now let's try this skill out.

Think of a recent troubling situation—something that caused you to feel irritated, annoyed, or stressed, for example. On a scale from 0 (no emotion) to 10 (most intense emotion imaginable), the feeling should be around a 3 or 4. Imagine that situation now as best as you can so that you experience the emotion. Once you feel it, close your eyes, if that's comfortable for you, and go to your secure place. Picture it in your mind, and let yourself be there, allowing yourself to experience the calm, peace, and security of that place. Stay with that image as long as you'd like, and see if you can get those emotions back down to a 1 or even 0.

Hopefully you saw your emotions come back down. And don't forget that you can use other skills in conjunction with the secure place, as well. For example, if your emotion is intense, you might need to do some reregulating before you can use your secure place. This rescue skill is just another tool to provide you with emotional relief!

Wrapping Up

In this chapter you learned a lot about relationships: why they're necessary, how to increase the number you have if you don't have enough, and how to make the ones you do have healthier. We also looked at how to end unhealthy relationships. As you worked through the chapter, hopefully you considered your own relationships and how these skills might apply to you.

In the next and final chapter we'll discuss putting together all of the skills you've learned, and you'll learn a couple more skills to help ensure your success in getting relief from your emotions moving forward. I hope you're continuing to take your time to really absorb and put into practice what you've been learning in this workbook, so that you can make meaningful and lasting changes in your life. When you're ready, turn the page and move on to our final chapter.

CHAPTER 10

Next Steps

When you struggle with emotion dysregulation, you might find that your life feels overwhelming and unmanageable at times. You might be in a constant state of stress, doing things to damage important relationships, and beating yourself up, reducing your self-respect and self-esteem, all of which can add up over time to more severe negative consequences. In essence, emotion dysregulation makes it difficult to get to where you'd like to be in life. The skills you've learned in this workbook can help you get relief from your emotions and change all of that. It's not easy, of course, but if you've been practicing the skills you've learned, hopefully you're already starting to see changes, even if they're small.

In this final chapter, I'm going to help you build on that momentum. First, we'll assess how you're doing with the skills you've learned, and then we'll turn to next steps. We'll put a plan in place to help you continue using skills to manage your emotions in healthier ways (or to start using skills if you've been struggling with practicing), and we'll look at one final rescue skill.

Where Are You Now?

One thing I've stressed throughout this workbook is the importance of self-awareness in making changes. So, let's look at where you are now before we figure out what your next steps are.

Self-Assessment

Answer the following questions as honestly as you can. If a question has an answer that's discouraging, or that you don't like for some reason, that's okay; accept whatever the reality is, write out the honest (non-judgmental!) answer, and move on to the next question.

Have you made any changes in your life since you began this work? For example, have your target behaviors decreased or increased? Have you noticed changes in thoughts and feelings about yourself? Or changes in relationships?

_____

_____

_____

Have others commented on changes they've seen in you, even if you haven't seen them yourself? If so, write them here.

_____

_____

_____

Whether or not you've seen changes, have you learned anything about yourself in doing this work? (Perhaps you discovered some goals for yourself, things that would make your life more fulfilling, or identified changes you'd like to make in relationships.)

_____

_____

_____

Have you found a particular skill (or several) especially helpful, or has one resonated with you in some way? (If you haven't been able to bring yourself to practice skills yet, perhaps you can see that certain skills will be helpful for you.) Write your thoughts here.

_____

_____

_____

Reflecting on the work you've done, what do you think you need to do to move yourself in the direction of positive change, to maintain the changes you've made, or to improve upon the changes you've made? Write anything that comes to mind. (And if nothing comes to mind, don't worry; I'm going to help with that!)

_____

_____

_____

If you got stuck on some of these questions, don't worry, this is just the start of figuring out what your next steps are. The analysis we'll look at next will provide you with a concrete tool to help you figure it out.

The Solution Analysis of Problem Behavior

The Solution Analysis of Problem Behavior is a follow-up to the Behavioral Analysis (BA) we looked at in chapter 1. If you've been working on these BAs, you know how they help you analyze your behavior to get a better understanding of what's triggering it, and of the thoughts, emotions, behaviors, and events involved in moving you from the prompting event to the target behavior.

The Solution Analysis of Problem Behavior builds on the BAs, helping you use the insight gleaned from them to change your behavior in future. I provided a sample solution analysis for you based on Charlie's BA on emotional eating from chapter 1, followed by a blank form. You can download more of these blank forms at this book's website: http://www.newharbinger.com/49647.

Solution Analysis of Problem Behavior

Ways to reduce my *vulnerability* in the future:

- Increase my self-care so I can manage my stress better: hiking, yoga, reading, reaching out to friends more (look at my distress tolerance skills list for more ideas).
- Plan better when I have time off and make sure I follow through with my plans by scheduling activities.
- Keep healthy snack foods in the house and buy less of the foods I'm more likely to overeat (until I get my urges more under control).

Ways to prevent the *prompting event* from happening again. (We don't always have control over this, but see what ideas you can come up with.)

- I can't prevent Mom from leaving messages that make me feel guilty, but I can use my assertiveness skills to remind her that I don't want contact with her and the family right now.

Ways to work on interrupting the *links* in the chain between the *prompting event* and the *problem behavior*. (How can you interrupt the links in the chain so you'll be less likely to engage in the problem behavior next time?)

- When I saw that my mom had called, I could have postponed listening to her message because I knew that it was likely to trigger me. When I listened to the message and felt guilty, I could have reminded myself right then that it's a wise mind choice for me to take time away from my family, and guilt isn't justified (using wise mind, dialectical thinking).
- Nonjudgmental stance with my self-judgments.
- Radical acceptance: this is who my mom is, and what she does.
- Dialectical thinking: I know she doesn't do this on purpose, this is the same way her mom treated her.
- I need to work on validating my anger toward my mom. This will also help reduce my guilt, which is a secondary emotion.
- To help with my feelings of being overwhelmed I could have done a reregulating skill (stuck my face in cold water, forward bend, paced breathing).
- Urge management: as soon as I noticed the urge to eat, I could have set a timer for fifteen minutes and pulled out my list of distress tolerance skills and started using them.
- Mindfulness might also have helped—mindfulness of my thoughts and feelings. If I do start to eat, eating mindfully would help me be aware of when I've had enough.

> Are there things that you need to do to correct or repair the harm caused by the problem behavior?
>
> - No harm was caused to anyone else, just to myself. I could offer repair to myself by committing to healthier eating habits and getting back to my regular exercise routine that I've fallen out of, as well as just generally treating myself better emotionally and physically (stretching, nonjudgmental stance, self–validation).

Now it's your turn. Considering all you've learned in this workbook, complete a Solution Analysis of Problem Behavior on one of your target behaviors. Remember to work on one at a time; if you've done BAs on multiple behaviors, choose one behavior to start with and return to the others once you've seen some progress in eliminating the problem behavior.

Solution Analysis of Problem Behavior

Ways to reduce my *vulnerability* in the future:

Ways to prevent the *prompting event* from happening again. (We don't always have control over this, but see what ideas you can come up with.)

Ways to work on interrupting the *links* in the chain between the *prompting event* and the *problem behavior*. (How can you interrupt the links in the chain so you'll be less likely to engage in the problem behavior next time?)

Are there things that you need to do to correct or repair the harm caused by the problem behavior?

Planning for a Skillful Future

Now we're going to put all of the skills and information you've learned together. You'll find that the skills you've learned in this workbook start to come naturally over time, but to get there you have to continue to put the energy into practicing. This next skill will help you do that.

Writing a Letter to Yourself

Having an encouraging, compassionate coach can help motivate you to practice skills, and in the case of emotion dysregulation, that coach needs to be you. In the space provided, write a letter from your wise self to your "emotionally dysregulated self" (or whatever term fits best for you)—in other words, to that part of you still struggling to manage emotions in healthy, balanced ways (or perhaps still struggling to even *want* to!). Ask your wise self, *What does that dysregulated self need?* When emotions get intense and you have urges to go back to a target behavior or turn to new ones to manage the pain, how can you help yourself use skills instead of falling back into old patterns? You might find it helpful to review the questions you answered in the self-assessment at the beginning of this chapter, and if you need more room, grab another piece of paper.

_____

_____

_____

_____

_____

_____

_____

_____

_____

You might want to return later to write this letter if now isn't the right time—for instance, if you're really struggling with emotions right now, or if you're feeling willful. It can also be a good idea to come back to this letter periodically to update it, writing about new things you've accomplished or new skills you've discovered that help you in certain situations.

Rescue Skill: Your Letter

Once you've written your letter, figure out a place to put it where it will be accessible whenever you need it. This letter can be another helpful tool to bring you fast relief when emotions get intense, reminding you of skills to practice, as well as of the reasons you have for doing this hard work, and providing you with that nonjudgmental perspective.

You might put your letter in your phone or tablet so you always have it with you; if privacy isn't an issue, you might write it out for yourself and hang it on your wall or even frame it. Whatever you do with it, be sure to add it to your distress tolerance skills list (see chapter 2). It's also important to read this letter to yourself not just when you start to notice heightened emotions or a problematic urge, but regularly as a reminder of the positive changes you've made and are continuing to strive toward—in other words, reactively and proactively!

Cope Ahead

Did you know that our brain can't tell the difference between something that's real and something that's imagined? It's why we have the emotion of *anxiety,* which is when we worry about something that hasn't happened. But this aspect of our brain can also work to our benefit, because it means we can practice skills in our imagination. Practicing skills before we need to use them in real time, or with situations that may occur, will improve our performance when the stakes are higher. This is where the DBT skill of cope ahead (Linehan 2014) can come in handy.

When can you use cope ahead? When you're new to DBT skills and you want to practice them to get more proficient, you can use cope ahead to imagine the difficulties you're anticipating and envision yourself using your new skills. When you want to practice using a skill in a situation that's new to you. When you're facing a situation that's causing strong emotions that may interfere with your ability to use distress tolerance skills. When you want to ensure the best possible outcome in a situation. In other words, you can use the cope ahead skill whenever you want, and doing so will enhance your performance when you're facing a difficult situation in reality. Here's how to do it:

1. Describe the situation you expect to be a problem. What's the worst-case scenario, or the catastrophe, you're imagining? For example, let's say you want to have a difficult

conversation with your partner to observe a limit with them. What are you worried will happen? Is it that you'll have a fight? That they'll give you the silent treatment for days? Or that they'll be so hurt and angry that they'll end the relationship? (Just *naming* what you're afraid of is often helpful, as you can then sometimes see how completely unrealistic that fear is!)

2. Next, imagine that worst-case scenario actually happens. (Let's face it, most of us are pretty good at this part!) Which skills would you use to help you cope? Using the previous worst-case scenario, for example, if your partner is ending the relationship, what skills would you use to help yourself through that difficult situation? You would probably want to reach out to friends and family for support, practice accepting reality, act opposite to your emotions (perhaps with the hurt and anger you feel toward your ex-partner, perhaps with the love you feel to help reduce those feelings over time), and use reregulating and distracting skills. There are likely many skills you can think of that would be helpful in a situation like this; write them down so you don't forget them.

3. The final step is to practice: Imagine yourself in that worst-case scenario, using the skills you've come up with and being effective. This will build your confidence, teaching you that you know how to deal with the very worst outcome imaginable. And should things actually turn out that way (which they rarely do), you'll know exactly what to do. The other benefit of this skill is that we get better at what we practice. On the one hand, if we spend time ruminating about a worst-case scenario and getting stuck on how awful it will be, we're going to get better at ruminating and catastrophizing. If, on the other hand, we practice cope ahead, we'll get better at using our skills because of that imaginal practice.

This skill will be invaluable when it comes to improving your ability to regulate your emotions. The question with all of these skills, however, is *Are you willing to practice?*

Getting Back to Willingness

In chapter 7 we discussed *willingness*, being open to possibilities, and *willfulness*, which is when we give up, stop trying, close ourselves off to possibilities, and do everything we can to avoid feeling something. We all experience willfulness at times. I'm sure you can think of a time when life kept throwing problem after problem at you and you threw up your hands and stopped trying to problem solve. When people struggle with emotion dysregulation, they often go through periods during which they just want to pretend that "everything's fine" and not put so much energy into their emotions every day. It makes sense that sometimes you'll choose not to use the skills you've learned because they're hard, and you won't always have the energy to devote to making changes.

So when you notice that willfulness has arisen, do your best to get back to a more willing place; this will increase the likelihood that you'll stay on track (or get on track) with the skills you learned in this workbook. Here's how:

1. Accept that willfulness is here. Just observe: *I'm feeling willful right now.*

2. Use your favorite skills to reregulate, such as the forward bend or sticking your face in cold water.

3. Change your body language by taking an open posture and using the half smile to get to a more willing place.

If you've tried these things and you're still feeling willful, ask yourself, *What is it that I'm afraid of?* Anxiety often maintains willfulness. For instance, you might find yourself worrying about how you'll manage without the problem behavior you're trying to eliminate, or what expectations might be put on you if you're managing your emotions better. Figuring out what the threat is (Linehan 2014) can help you get to a place of willingness, from where you'll be able to bring other skills to bear to help you be more effective.

Since self-talk influences emotions, notice how you're talking to yourself about the changes you're trying to make. Instead of reminding yourself of how awful things are or how difficult something is, or berating yourself when you don't achieve a goal, try cheerleading yourself. You might want to write out a list of encouraging statements you can read when you're struggling: for example, "Yes, it's hard, but I'm going to keep working at it, and over time I'll get there."

Be Willing to Ask for Help

Asking for help is not a sign of weakness! And I'm fairly certain that the people who are important to you will not only be happy to help if you ask, but they'll be happy to know that you're working on managing your emotions more effectively. The skills in this workbook could benefit the people in your life as well, so lend them this book, or teach them a specific skill that resonates with you or that you need help with. Let them know what you'd like them to do to help you (for example, reminding you to do a forward bend to help you get to your wise mind, or pointing out when you're not thinking dialectically). Keep in mind, of course, that if you *ask* for help, you have to be willing to accept the help that's offered, so don't get angry at your loved ones when they're doing what you've asked of them.

Wrapping Up

Changing how you manage emotions is typically a long road. If you've been stuck in a dysregulated pattern for a lifetime, remind yourself that it's unlikely that life changes will happen in an instant. As difficult as this work can be, have patience with yourself, keep working at it, and you *will* create a happier and healthier life. It will be worth it in the long run. So, what do you think? Are you willing?

References

Aron, E. N. 2016. *The Highly Sensitive Person: How to Thrive When the World Overwhelms You.* New York: Broadway Books.

Beil, K., and D. Hanes. 2013. "The Influence of Urban Natural and Built Environments on Physiological and Psychological Measures of Stress—A Pilot Study." *International Journal of Environmental Research and Public Health* 10 (4): 1250–67.

Bernstein, E. E., and R. J. McNally. 2017. "Acute Aerobic Exercise Helps Overcome Emotion Regulation Deficits." *Cognition and Emotion* 31 (4): 834.

Dolgoff-Kaspar R., A. Baldwin, M. S. Johnson, N. Edling, and G. K. Sethi. 2012. "Effect of Laughter Yoga on Mood and Heart Rate Variability in Patients Awaiting Organ Transplantation: A Pilot Study." *Alternative Therapies in Health and Medicine* 18 (5): 61–66.

Ekman, P., and R. J. Davidson. 1993. "Voluntary Smiling Changes Regional Brain Activity." *Psychological Science* 4 (5): 342–45.

Emmons, R. A., and M. E. McCullough. 2003. "Counting Blessings Versus Burdens: An Experimental Investigation of Gratitude and Subjective Well-Being in Daily Life." *Journal of Personality and Social Psychology* 84 (2): 377–89.

Germer, C. K. 2009. *The Mindful Path to Self-Compassion: Freeing Yourself from Destructive Thoughts and Emotions.* New York: Guilford Press.

Heutz, R. 2017. "Can Mindfulness Beat Alzheimer's Disease?" *Maastricht Journal of Liberal Arts* 9: 33–48.

Holt-Lunstad, J., T. B. Smith, M. Baker, T. Harris, and D. Stephenson. 2015. "Loneliness and Social Isolation as Risk Factors for Mortality: A Meta-Analytic Review." *Perspectives on Psychological Science* 10 (2): 227–37.

Koole, S. L. 2009. "The Psychology of Emotion Regulation: An Integrative Review." *Cognition and Emotion* 23 (1): 4–41.

Linehan, M. M. 1993. *Cognitive-Behavioral Treatment of Borderline Personality Disorder.* New York: Guilford Press.

Linehan, M. M. 2000. *Opposite Action: Changing Emotions You Want to Change.* Seattle: Behavioral Tech.

Linehan, M. M. 2003a. *From Chaos To Freedom. Getting Through a Crisis Without Making It Worse: Crisis Survival Skills: Part Two—Improving the Moment and Pros and Cons.* Seattle: Behavioral Tech.

Linehan, M. M. 2003b. *From Chaos To Freedom. Getting Through a Crisis Without Making It Worse: Crisis Survival Skills: Part One—Distracting and Self-Soothing.* Seattle: Behavioral Tech.

Linehan, M. M. 2003c. *From Chaos To Freedom. From Suffering To Freedom: Practicing Reality Acceptance.* Seattle: Behavioral Tech.

Linehan, M. M. 2005. *From Chaos To Freedom. This One Moment: Skills for Everyday Mindfulness.* Seattle: Behavioral Tech.

Linehan, M. M. 2014. *DBT Skills Training Manual.* 2nd ed. New York: Guilford Press.

May, G. G. 1982. *Will and Spirit: A Contemplative Psychology.* New York: HarperCollins.

Sheldon, K. M., and S. Lyubomirsky. 2007. "How to Increase and Sustain Positive Emotion: The Effects of Expressing Gratitude and Visualizing Best Possible Selves." *Journal of Positive Psychology* 1 (2): 73–82.

Shipon, R. W. 2007. "Gratitude: Effect on Perspectives and Blood Pressure of Inner-City African-American Hypertensive Patients." *Dissertation Abstracts International: Section B: The Sciences and Engineering,* 68 (3-B), 1977.

Siegel, D. 2014. *Brainstorm: The Power and Purpose of the Teenage Brain.* New York: Jeremy P. Tarcher/Penguin.

Van Dijk, S. 2012. *Calming the Emotional Storm: Using Dialectical Behavior Therapy Skills to Manage Your Emotions and Balance Your Life.* Oakland, CA: New Harbinger Publications.

Van Dijk, S. 2013. *DBT Made Simple: A Step-by-Step Guide to Dialectical Behavior Therapy.* Oakland, CA: New Harbinger Publications.

Van Dijk, S. 2021. *The DBT Skills Workbook for Teen Self-Harm.* Oakland, CA: New Harbinger Publications.

Wood, A. M., S. Joseph, J. Lloyd, and S. Atkins. 2009. "Gratitude Influences Sleep Through the Mechanism of Pre-Sleep Cognitions." *Journal of Psychosomatic Research* 66 (1): 43–48.

Sheri Van Dijk, MSW, is a psychotherapist, and renowned dialectical behavior therapy (DBT) expert. She is author of several books, including *Calming the Emotional Storm, Don't Let Your Emotions Run Your Life for Teens,* and *The Self-Harm Workbook for Teens.* Her books focus on using DBT skills to help people manage their emotions and cultivate lasting well-being. She is also the recipient of the R.O. Jones Award from the Canadian Psychiatric Association.

FROM OUR COFOUNDER—

As cofounder of New Harbinger and a clinical psychologist since 1978, I know that emotional problems are best helped with evidence-based therapies. These are the treatments derived from scientific research (randomized controlled trials) that show what works. Whether these treatments are delivered by trained clinicians or found in a self-help book, they are designed to provide you with proven strategies to overcome your problem.

Therapies that aren't evidence-based—whether offered by clinicians or in books—are much less likely to help. In fact, therapies that aren't guided by science may not help you at all. That's why this New Harbinger book is based on scientific evidence that the treatment can relieve emotional pain.

This is important: if this book isn't enough, and you need the help of a skilled therapist, use the following resources to find a clinician trained in the evidence-based protocols appropriate for your problem. And if you need more support—a community that understands what you're going through and can show you ways to cope—resources for that are provided below, as well.

Real help is available for the problems you have been struggling with. The skills you can learn from evidence-based therapies will change your life.

Matthew McKay, PhD
Cofounder, New Harbinger Publications

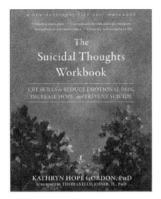

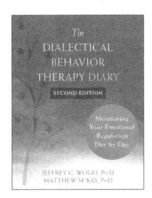
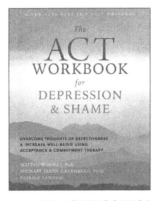
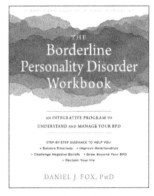

Did you know there are **free tools** you can download for this book?

Free tools are things like **worksheets, guided meditation exercises**, and **more** that will help you get the most out of your book.

You can download free tools for this book—whether you bought or borrowed it, in any format, from any source—from the New Harbinger website. All you need is a NewHarbinger.com account. Just use the URL provided in this book to view the free tools that are available for it. Then, click on the "download" button for the free tool you want, and follow the prompts that appear to log in to your NewHarbinger.com account and download the material.

You can also save the free tools for this book to your **Free Tools Library** so you can access them again anytime, just by logging in to your account! Just look for this button on the book's free tools page.

+ Save this to my free tools library

If you need help accessing or downloading free tools, visit **newharbinger.com/faq** or contact us at **customerservice@newharbinger.com**.